Mountains
In the
Valley

Selected Poetry

Marcia Y. Collins

© 2018 Marcia Y. Collins

All rights reserved. No part of this book may be reproduced or transmitted in any form or by any means, electronic or mechanical, or by any information or storage and retrieval system without permission in writing from the author.

Please Note: Biblical references came from several sources, including Internet websites, and as versions differ slightly may not be an exact match to the Bible of your choice.

Cover photograph © Sheila Ruffin

Cover and interior design and layout by Yolanda Ciolli

AKA-Publishing.com/Compass Flower Press
Columbia, Missouri

ISBN: 978-1-942168-91-1
Trade Paperback

Dedication

To my children: Quentin, Nicholas, and Danielle,
who, in spite of trials faced in life have had
the courage to persevere and not lose hope.
Their resilience has encouraged me to do the same.

Contents

Dedication _____ 3
All I Need _____ 9
Just Us _____ 10
On Time _____ 11
Praise the Lord _____ 12
Unshakable _____ 13
God Is Good _____ 14
Joy _____ 15
Greater Than the Odds _____ 16
Peace! Be Still! _____ 17
Rise and Shine _____ 18
Restoration _____ 19
Peace _____ 20
Day by Day _____ 21
Purpose _____ 22
Home Going _____ 23
In Due Season _____ 24
Stay in the Word _____ 25
Labor and Reward _____ 26
Moving On _____ 27
Creation _____ 28
Gentleness _____ 29
In My Skin _____ 30
Forgiven _____ 32
Doing Good _____ 33
Hope Beyond Sin _____ 34
Testimony _____ 35
Happy New Year _____ 36
Waiting Wondering Wishing _____ 37
The Secret Place _____ 38
From You I Learn _____ 39
The Competition _____ 40
Healing Prayer _____ 41
Granny-Style _____ 42
Follow Through _____ 43
The Life I Live _____ 44

All in a Day	45
My New Red Coat	46
Into the Deep	47
Moving Day	48
God Is There	49
Remember Not to Forget	50
Listen	51
Doing My Best	52
Meekness	53
Oversight	54
Control	56
Changed	57
Righteousness and Works	58
Tribute	60
Holding on to Hope	61
Grief	62
Just My Imagination	63
Seek ME; Find ME	64
A Voice in the Valley	65
Oh Valentine, So True	66
Live for Today	67
Sanctuary	68
Just in Time	69
Dear Son	70
Wake Up	71
GOD	72
Get Over It	73
Faith	74
In His Hands	75
Religion, Relationship, and Church	76
God Is	78
Detours	79
Remembering Mama	80
Transition	81
All You Need	82
From Heaven to Earth	83
Impressions	84

In His Image	85
Soul Rage	86
Keep On Keeping Me	87
The Real Deal	88
Night Lights	89
A Good Return	90
Every Step of the Way	91
My Source, My All	92
Going Forward	93
Praise Worthy	94
Practice Makes Perfect	95
Who You Gonna Call?	96
Nothing to Lose	97
On Bended Knee	98
Faithful	99
From Wilderness to Wonder	100
It's the Law	101
An Appointed Time	102
Satisfied in HIM	103
Fine Tune	104
Higher Ground	105
The Beautiful Gate	106
A New Direction	108
A Family Affair	109
Vessels	110
Emotions	111
Charlie	112
Changing of the Guard	114
Who Else but GOD?	115
Refuge	116
Choices	117
Heed and Succeed	118
As Jesus Would	119
It Is Written	120
Love for Life	121
Stay in the Sheepfold	122
Wait and See	123

A Lesson of Love	124
The Voice of Wisdom	125
True Wealth	126
Hope in Loss	127
The Bridge	128
Silent Plea	129
Mighty Avenger	130
Never Alone	131
Content in HIM	132
Let HIM Drive	133
Words	134
Any Given Moment	135
Motherhood	136
While You Wait	137
Church Lady	138
Intercession	140
Good as New	141
The Man in the Median	142
A Friend in Deed	143
Diving into Destiny	144
No Offense	145
Choices and Voices	146
Wisdom and Revelation	148
Girlfriends	149
Service with a Smile	150
About Easter	152
Good Friday	154
The Tongue	156
Crossing Over	157
More Than You See	158
Our Help	159
Hidden Treasure	160
Mercy	161
About the Author	163
Acknowledgments	165

All I Need

The Lord is my defender,
A great, invincible force.
He provides for all my needs.
I receive without remorse.
The arm of the flesh is weak,
But my God is very strong.
Why look to another
When He can do no wrong?

"But let all those rejoice who put their trust in You; let them ever shout for joy, because You defend them; let those also who love Your name be joyful in You. For You, O Lord, will bless the righteous; with favor You will surround him as with a shield." Psalm 5:11-12

Just Us

When justice goes awry,
We all should wonder why.
"An eye for an eye, a tooth for a tooth"
Has become a horrid, distorted truth.
But how many eyes and how many teeth
Must this generation bequeath?
Are we not tired of these senseless acts
That leave our sons dead, on their backs?
In our weariness, what will we do?
Is there a voice that speaks to you?
Tears flow like a river as I sing a sad song,
Reflecting on right going terribly wrong.

"O Lord, how long shall I cry, and You will not hear? Even cry out to You, "Violence!" And You will not save. Why do You show me iniquity, and cause me to see trouble? For plundering and violence are before me; there is strife, and contention arises. Therefore the law is powerless, and justice never goes forth. For the wicked surround the righteous; therefore perverse judgment proceeds." Habakkuk 1:2-4

On Time

As I learn to wait upon the Lord,
He will renew my strength.
I need not be discouraged
When my wait seems at great length.
The Lord is ever mindful of me;
His delay does not mean denial.
I simply must learn to trust in Him
Through every test and trial!

"Even the youths shall faint and be weary, and the young men shall utterly fall: But they that wait upon the Lord shall renew their strength; they shall mount up with wings as eagles; they shall run, and not be weary; they shall walk, and not faint." Isaiah 40:30-31

Praise the Lord

Praise the Lord,
Our Sovereign King!
Praise the Lord,
Who made everything!
No one is higher;
No one can reach lower;
No one is greater;
He has all power!
Praise the Lord,
The giver of salvation!
Praise the Lord,
The healer for all nations!

"Make a joyful shout to God, all the earth! Sing out the honor of His name; make His praise glorious. Say to God, 'How awesome are Your works! Through the greatness of Your power Your enemies shall submit themselves to You. All the earth shall worship You and sing praises to You; they shall sing praises to Your name.' Selah." Psalm 66:1-4

Unshakable

In sickness and health, more than enough or nothing to spare,
Through the highs and lows of life, God is there.
When we are weak, He is strong.
When we let go, He holds on.
He is not swayed by our doubt.
He has a plan to bring us out
From despair into His marvelous light.
His Spirit brings comfort in the midst of blight.
So when the dawn brings a new day,
Take courage and know God has made a way.

"Be strong and of good courage, do not fear nor be afraid of them; for the Lord your God, He is the One who goes with you. He will not leave you nor forsake you. And the Lord, He is the One who goes before you. He will be with you; He will not leave you nor forsake you; do not fear nor be dismayed." Deuteronomy 31:6, 8

God Is Good

God is good.
He loves us.
He longs for relationship with us.
He wants to bless us.
He waits for us to cry out to Him.
He answers us.
God is good!

God is good.
Every good thing comes from Him.
He is our sun, an everlasting light.
He is our shield to protect us from harm.
He changes not, be it yesterday, today, or forever.
He will never leave us.
His grace, mercy, and longsuffering draw us to repentance.
He is our hope.
God is good!

"For the Lord God is a sun and shield; the Lord will give grace and glory; no good thing will He withhold from those who walk uprightly. O Lord of hosts, blessed is the man who trusts in You!" Psalm 84:11-12

Joy

Joy gives you hope in the time of sorrow.
Joy gives you strength to endure.
With joy, there is reason to yearn for tomorrow
Though the future is somewhat obscure.
Joy makes you laugh when you want to cry.
Joy keeps the heart warm.
Joy helps you trust when others ask why
And brings peace in a raging storm!

"Blessed be the LORD, because He has heard the voice of my supplication. The LORD is my strength and my shield; my heart trusts in Him, and I am helped; therefore my heart greatly rejoices, and with my song I will praise Him. The Lord is the strength of His people; and He is the saving refuge of His anointed." Psalm 28:6-8

Greater Than the Odds

How can you say who I am, what I will do, or who I will be?
How can you tell what potential is dwelling inside of me?

You can only see the shell of a person when you stand afar and gaze.
Take a moment to learn their story before you judge their ways.

Not one of us sets out in life to fail or barely get by.
The odds are sometimes against us, no matter how hard we try.

But even with adverse circumstance, there comes a time to move on.
Look to the God who created us and hasten to His throne.

In His presence there is mercy, along with strength we need
To overcome our failures and gain wisdom to succeed!

"As you come to Him, a living stone rejected by men but in the sight of God chosen and precious, you yourselves like living stones are being built up as a spiritual house, to be a holy priesthood, to offer spiritual sacrifices acceptable to God through Jesus Christ. But you are a chosen race, a royal priesthood, a holy nation, a people for His own possession, that you may proclaim the praises of Him who called you out of darkness into His marvelous light. Once you were not a people, but now you are God's people; once you had not received mercy, but now you have received mercy." 1 Peter 2:4-5; 9-10

Peace! Be Still!

Sometimes
On the sea of life
The sailing is not so smooth!
Fierce winds hasten
To alter our course.
Somber skies and murky clouds
Disrupt our heavenly view.
Tempestuous waves emerge
To prevail against our souls.
Yet as the abyss would have its way
To utterly destroy,
We cry out to our God,
And the angels are dispatched
To hold back the winds,
Disband the clouds,
And turn dark skies to blue;
To still the raging sea
And restore peace to our souls!

"The Lord has established His throne in heaven, and His kingdom rules over all. Bless the Lord, you His angels, who excel in strength, that do His commandments, hearkening unto the voice of His word. Bless the Lord, all you His hosts, you ministers of His, who do His pleasure. Bless the Lord, all His works, in all places of His dominion. Bless the Lord, O my soul!" Psalm 103:19-22

Rise and Shine

Many thoughts run through my mind
As I begin my daily grind.
Thankful to see a new sunrise,
But wish I had more time to lie.
Pull back the covers; no time to waste.
Step lively now; no need to be late!
Finally dressed and out the door,
Wondering what the day holds in store.
I pray it is good, whatever it may be,
And that angels stay close to watch over me.

"Let me hear in the morning of Your steadfast love, for in You I trust. Make me know the way I should go, for to You I lift up my soul." Psalm 143:8

Restoration

Lord, send the rain, refreshing and pure.
Renew my strength and help me endure.
As I seek You and delight in Your ways,
Please hasten the dawn of better days.
No more sorrow, no more pain,
Only the former and latter rain
To wash away the years of drought
And send a harvest so I am never without.

"Be glad then, you children of Zion, and rejoice in the Lord, your God; for He gives you the former or early rain in just measure and in righteousness, and He causes to come down for you the rain, the former rain and the latter rain, as before. The threshing floors shall be full of grain and the vats shall overflow with new wine and oil. And I will restore to you the years that the locust has eaten, the cankerworm, and the caterpillar, and the palmerworm, My great army which I sent among you. And you shall eat in plenty and be satisfied and praise the name of the LORD your God, Who has dealt wondrously with you; and My people shall never be ashamed." Joel 2:23-26

Peace

Peace to surpass understanding
Is what You have promised to give.
In the world there is great tribulation,
But Your peace renders grace to live,
And even in the midst of sorrow,
When our hearts are filled with grief,
As we place our hope in You,
Your peace brings the soul relief.

"The Lord bless you and keep you; the Lord make His face to shine upon you, and be gracious unto you; the Lord lift His countenance upon you, and give you peace." Numbers 6:24-26

Day by Day

Yesterday is gone,
Never to return;
Today is the present
We did not earn.
Tomorrow is the future,
A day we plan to see,
But even though we plan,
There is no guarantee.
So thank God for the day
That is before you now,
And if another comes,
You need not wonder how.

"Come now, you who say, today or tomorrow we will go into such a city, and continue there a year, and buy and sell, and get gain; whereas you do not know what will happen tomorrow. For what is your life? It is even a vapor that appears for a little time and then vanishes away. Instead you ought to say, If the Lord will, we shall live, and do this, or that." James 4:13-15

Purpose

As you journey on the pathway of life,
You will find there is a work to be done.
Moments of pleasure are good to the soul,
But there is more to living than fun.
We were all created for a purpose
And have a charge to fulfill.
Do not allow setbacks to deter you
Or get sidetracked by a fleeting thrill.
As you live, the day is sure to come
You will sense God beckoning you
To come into the Body of Christ
And learn what you are called to do.
He is more than able to equip you
For whatever your task may demand,
So on that Day of Judgment,
With confidence, you can stand!

"For you were once darkness, but now, you are light in the Lord. Walk as children of light, for the fruit of the light results in all goodness, righteousness, and truth, finding out what is acceptable to the Lord. Have no fellowship with the unfruitful works of darkness, but rather expose them; for it is shameful even to speak of those things which are done by them in secret. Everything exposed by the light is made clear, for what makes everything clear is light. Therefore He says: Awake, you who sleep; arise from the dead, and Christ will give you light. Pay careful attention, then, to how you walk, not as unwise people but as wise, making the most of the time, because the days are evil. Therefore do not be unwise, but understand what the will of the Lord is." Ephesians 5:8-17

Home Going

Spending time with family and friends
Was bitter sweet today.
We said goodbye to a loved one,
Who unexpectedly passed away.
The church was packed with many who cared
With numerous stories to tell.
Truly a testament of the life
She endeavored to live so well.
The singers sang melodious tunes
Familiar to the ear.
The message throughout the service
Resounded loud and clear:
Hazel Rozetta Lewis,
Her journey on earth is complete.
While here, she learned how to live holy,
So the Savior she would meet.
And now, the task before us
Is to learn how to do the same,
So we can hear the Savior
Joyfully calling our names!

"Let not your heart be troubled; you believe in God, believe also in Me. In my Father's house are many mansions; if it were not so, I would have told you. I go to prepare a place for you. And if I go and prepare a place for you, I will come again and receive you to Myself; that where I am, there you may be also." John 14:1-3

In Due Season

As we see others prosper,
While waiting to receive,
We must not grow weary;
Instead, trust and believe.
For as time passes by,
There is no need to fret.
When God makes a promise,
He will never forget!

"Know therefore that the Lord your God is God, the faithful God, who keeps His promise and shows steadfast love with those who love Him and keep His commandments, to a thousand generations." Deuteronomy 7:9

Stay in the Word

There is always some form of work
We need to get done.
Occasionally, instead of work,
We choose to have fun.
However, what is needful
As we go about each day,
Is finding time to rest in the Lord,
Study His word, and pray.
We cannot live by bread alone;
This only feeds the flesh.
We have to know the word of God,
So spirit and soul will mesh.
For if the flesh grows stronger,
While the spirit becomes weak,
Our souls will be left to wander,
For pleasures they should not seek!

"My child, pay attention to what I say; listen closely to my words. Don't let them out of your sight. Never stop thinking about them. These words are the secret of life and health to all who discover them. Above all, be careful what you think because your thoughts control your life." Proverbs 4:20-23

Labor and Reward

When I chase God, His blessings chase me!
I don't even have to look around to see
If they are coming, for I know they are.
He's been too good, and He's brought me too far.
There's just no use to turn back now;
I'm keeping my hand on the gospel plow!
Cultivating soil wherever I go,
By sharing God's word, so others will grow.

"The blessing of the LORD, it makes rich, and He adds no sorrow with it." Proverbs 10:22

Moving On

Mistakes…
I've made more than a few.
Oftentimes, the thought of them
Has made me cry the blues.

But crying doesn't change the fact
That what's been done is done.
I must move on, forget the past,
For my race is yet to be won.

It won't be easy to complete
The goals I want to achieve.
But I can do great things
If in myself I believe.

For I am more than a conqueror
Through Jesus Christ, my Lord.
He is the One who strengthens me
When trials seem too hard.

His grace is sufficient to handle
Whatever comes my way.
I shall reap a harvest of blessings
When in His will I stay!

"Who shall separate us from the love of Christ? Shall tribulation, or distress, or persecution, or famine, or nakedness, or peril, or sword? Yet in all these things we are more than conquerors through Him who loved us." Romans 8:35, 37

Creation

I thank God for the gifts He has given me to share
To encourage other people and demonstrate His care.
For God is truly loving, generous, and kind.
The world in which we live, He created with us in mind.
He separated the waters, with a firmament in the sky;
An expanse we know as Heaven some call, "The Sweet By and By."
He gathered the waters together and formed them into seas,
Allowing dry land to emerge covered with grass, herbs, and trees.
Herbs with seed, trees with fruit, a spectacular sight to see,
Growing all over creation to nourish you and me!
In the heavens, great lights appeared, to distinguish night from day:
The moon and stars as we slumber, the sun for work and play.
Within the seas, broad and deep, an abundance of living things
Yielding food for the nations and treasures sought by kings.
Now, looking towards the sky, another amazing sight;
Winged creatures of every sort effortlessly take flight!
Here on the earth before us, we find the cattle and beasts;
Each creeping thing has a purpose, from the greatest to the least.
The final and crowning moment, in accordance with His plan,
God took from the earth He created and made Himself a man.
In the image of God we are fashioned, male and female the same.
He is worthy of glory and honor; His greatness, forever proclaim!

"And God said, "See, I have given you every herb that yields seed which is on the face of all the earth, and every tree whose fruit yields seed; to you it shall be for food. Also, to every beast of the earth, to every bird of the air, and to everything that creeps on the earth, in which there is life, I have given every green herb for food"; and it was so. Then God saw everything that He had made, and indeed it was very good..." Genesis 1:29-31

Gentleness

A gentle word offers peace
To someone who is feeling low;
A gentle touch provides comfort
When pain rocks you to and fro;
A gentle look can bring a smile
To one whose heart is bound;
A gentle ear to listen
Is good to have around.
Showing kindness to others
Is something we should do;
For what you decide to give
Will surely come back to you!

"Therefore, as we have opportunity, let us do good to all, especially to those who are of the household of faith." Galatians 6:10

In My Skin

In my skin,
I am who I am
And know no other way to be.

*In MY skin
I gave you a glimpse
Of who you are to be.*

In my skin
I feel trapped in a world
Where I am not free to be me.

*In MY skin,
I created you
To look and act like Me.*

In my skin,
I am not so sure
Who that person is.

*In MY skin,
There is no darkness;
I AM the truth and the light!*

In my skin,
Is there a right?
Every day feels like a pop quiz!

*In MY skin,
Do not be confused;
I can show you what is right.*

In my skin,
When people stare,
It causes me a great deal of pain.

*In MY skin,
I feel the brunt
Of every whisper and jeer.*

In my skin,
When I hear them laugh,
It fills me with utter disdain.

*In MY skin,
I sense the pain
That makes you shed each tear.*

In my skin,
Without a trial,
I am found guilty as sin.

*In MY skin,
I silence your guilt
And make your enemies behave.*

In my skin,
How do I fight
The battle that rages within?

*In MY skin,
I conquered death
And brought victory beyond the grave!*

In my skin,
Is there peace
To exchange for my grief?

*In MY skin,
I drew you close
And carried the weight of your sorrow.*

In my skin,
Is there a place
Where I can find relief?

*In MY skin,
I bring you hope
For a brighter tomorrow!*

"Surely He has borne our griefs and carried our sorrows; yet we esteemed Him stricken, smitten by God, and afflicted. But He was wounded for our transgressions, He was bruised for our iniquities; the chastisement for our peace was upon Him, and by His stripes we are healed. All we like sheep have gone astray; we have turned, every one, to his own way; and the Lord has laid on Him the iniquity of us all." Isaiah 53:4-6

Forgiven

The favor of God has come to me;
I am not the same as I used to be.
I have new joy that floods my soul
As His word restores and makes me whole.
I give thanks to God, for He alone
Has a grace for those who hasten to His throne,
Where His mercy abounds and is new every day,
And His glory shines to show me the way
That leads to salvation and eternal life,
So I can be free of guilt and strife.

"We then, as workers together with Him, also plead with you not to receive the grace of God in vain. For He says, "In the time of My favor I heard you, and in the day of salvation I helped you." I tell you, now is the time of God's favor; now is the day of salvation." 2 Corinthians 6:1-2

Doing Good

When help is perceived as harm,
Do not abandon the quest
Of reaching out to others
And striving to give your best.
For even the best intention
Can be misunderstood
And taken out of context
Though you only meant it for good.

"Do not neglect to do good and to share what you have, for such sacrifices are pleasing to God." Hebrews 13:16

Hope Beyond Sin

Sin without; sin within.
None are without; not even ten!
We have all worn the mask that attempts to disguise
Momentary indiscretions when we failed to be wise.
Try as we might, we all fall short,
But there is hope, so do not abort.
God knows our flaws and He has a plan
To rescue the perishing and redeem fallen man.
When we ask in faith and choose to believe,
The gift of salvation is ours to receive.
As we come to know Jesus as Savior and Lord,
We will gain a peace only He can afford!

"But to all who did receive Him, who believed in His name; He gave the right to become children of God, who were born, not of natural descent, nor of the will of the flesh, nor of the will of man; but of God." John 1:12-13

Testimony

When you have overcome your past
And have the power to stand at last,
Be willing to share where you have been
And do it with a great big grin.
Do not worry when people talk
About your life and former walk.
Give God the glory for making it through
And realize there is potential in you.
Praise Him for giving you strength to endure
And for His grace to help you live pure.

"Beloved, I beg you as sojourners and pilgrims, abstain from fleshly lusts which war against the soul, having your conduct honorable among the Gentiles, that when they speak against you as evildoers, they may, by your good works which they observe, glorify God in the day of visitation."
1 Peter 2:11-12

Happy New Year

Another day, a New Year. What will it bring?
Trials that vex me sore?
Or triumphs that make my heart soar?
I would certainly prefer the latter,
For the other is a different matter
That I would just as soon not experience;
Nor would I be found dangling over a fence.
Nay, make my election sure;
Follow Christ and live pure.
Is there a better choice
To ensure I live to rejoice?
Let the redeemed of the Lord say so!
Live in a way so all will know
Your mind and body belong to Him.
Be not subject to any carnal whim;
Rather, live with self-control,
So when the bell happens to toll,
Be it for you, or be it for me,
We are found where we ought to be:
In His will and not our own,
Dwelling in the safety zone
Where troubles dare not enter in,
Where we keep our distance from sin,
In the secret place of the Most High God,
Even when others consider you odd.
O sing and shout the victory
And praise Him from now to eternity!

"Now therefore fear the Lord, and serve Him in sincerity and in truth, and put away the gods which your fathers served on the other side of the flood, and in Egypt, and serve the Lord! And if it seems evil to you to serve the Lord, choose for yourselves this day whom you will serve, whether the gods which your fathers served that were on the other side of the flood, or the gods of the Amorites, in whose land you dwell: But as for me and my house, we will serve the Lord." Joshua 24:14-15

Waiting Wondering Wishing

Waiting on your change to come,
Wondering when it will,
Wishing it would hurry up,
Just tell yourself, "Be still!"
Keep trusting and obeying God.
He has a plan in mind.
And though you think the hour is late,
He is not at all behind.

"For the vision is yet for an appointed time and it hastens to the end [fulfillment]; it will not deceive or disappoint. Though it tarry, wait [earnestly] for it, because it will surely come; it will not be behindhand on its appointed day." Habakkuk 2:3

The Secret Place

Dwelling in God's secret place,
His shadow covers you.
He is a refuge and fortress
In each trial you go through.
God knows the best solution
To solve the problem at hand,
Free you from all worry,
And give you strength to stand.
Trust Him to deliver
And shield you from all harm.
In Him there is great peace;
No need for alarm.

"He who dwells in the secret place of the Most High shall abide under the shadow of the Almighty. I will say of the Lord, He is my refuge and my fortress: my God; in Him will I trust." Psalm 91:1-2

From You I Learn

O Lord, You are my strength and hope.
Please show me daily how to cope;
While I am asking, help me not to complain
About my minor aches and pains,
For there are others who truly have it worse,
Who are under the care of a doctor or nurse.
Certainly, I am thankful for your grace toward me;
What is coming to pass, I scarcely imagined would be.
You have me in such a poetic flow;
Where this is going I am curious to know.
Guess I will strap in and enjoy the ride
While I glean from wisdom found at Your side.
As I study Your word both day and night,
By divine inspiration, I will continue to write.

"[For I always pray to] the God of our Lord Jesus Christ, the Father of glory, that He may grant you a spirit of wisdom and revelation [of insight into mysteries and secrets] in the [deep and intimate] knowledge of Him, by having the eyes of your heart flooded with light, so that you can know and understand the hope to which He has called you, and how rich is His glorious inheritance in the saints (His set-apart ones), and [so that you can know and understand] what is the immeasurable and unlimited and surpassing greatness of His power in and for us who believe, as demonstrated in the working of His mighty strength." Ephesians 1:17-19

The Competition

Three ladies in a kitchen,
Each given equal time
To take key ingredients
And create something sublime.
One lady made a cake
With frosting fluffy and white.
Another made cookies,
Truly a baker's delight.
The last made a pie,
With fruit throughout the dish,
Topped with a flakey crust,
Better than any could wish.
Each lady beamed with pride
At the thought of what she had done,
Believing within her heart
If there was a prize, she had won.
Imagine their surprise
When the Judge ruled "No Contest;"
For what each one had created,
He deemed to be their best.
The moral of this story
Is simple as can be.
What you were created to do
May not be the same as me.
We all have certain abilities
To use for the common goal
Of leading others to Christ
For salvation of their souls.

"You are the light of the world. A city set on a hill cannot be hidden. Nor do people light a lamp and put it under a basket, but on a stand, and it gives light to all in the house. In the same way, let your light shine before others, so that they may see your good works and give glory to your Father who is in heaven." Matthew 5:14-16

Healing Prayer

Sickness, plague, and calamity,
Lord send these far away from me
And my loved ones in despair;
Surround us with your tender care;
Bring healing to each ailing frame
And strengthen now, in Jesus' name!

"Then they cried to the Lord in their trouble, and He delivered them from their distress. He sent out His word and healed them, and delivered them from their destruction. Let them thank the Lord for His steadfast love, for His wondrous works to the children of man!" Psalm 107:19-21

Granny-Style

I remember when I was just a little girl,
My Granny used a hot comb to straighten my curl.
She also spanked my behind a time or two
When I ran my mouth, talking like a fool.
I should have known better; older folks did not play,
Unlike some people raising children today:
"Now, honey, please stop or you'll be in time out;
Try to remember what we talked about."
Honey, please! Time out was used in a game!
"Don't make me have to wait if I call your name!"
Now that is more what I remember,
And I dare not mumble, whine, or whimper.
"Be quiet, before I give you a reason to cry!
Stop that noise and dry your eyes!"
I know some are reading this shaking their heads,
Wondering how I did not end up dead;
To be honest, those days were not so bad,
And I may have exaggerated just a tad,
But not so much to deviate from truth,
Since the rod of correction was a part of my youth.
It helped to form the person I am today,
For it taught me a lesson when going astray.

"Train up a child in the way he should go: and when he is old, he will not depart from it. Foolishness is bound in the heart of a child; but the rod of correction shall drive it far from him." Proverbs 22:6, 15

Follow Through

When you give your word and offer a deed,
Make sure you are not driven by greed,
And if you commit to performing a task,
No one should have to come and ask,
Begging, pleading, and twisting your arm,
Or try to sway you by use of charm.
And if someone gets an attitude,
Do not turn around and act as rude,
Talking about what you "ain't gonna" do
And how your "mama didn't raise no fool!"
Now really, does it take all that?
Do we have to give "tit for tat"?
I say nay; we can do better than this
To live in harmony and genial bliss.
Just try to see Christ in those you serve
Without focusing on what they deserve.

"And whatsoever you do, do it heartily, as to the Lord, and not unto men; knowing that of the Lord you shall receive the reward of the inheritance: for you serve the Lord Christ." Colossians 3:23-24

The Life I Live

You live your life,
To make your mark,
And pray you make it well.

For how you lived
And what you did
Is the story others will tell.

So walk upright
And live in a way
To be clearly understood.

Then people will know
You did your best
To promote the common good.

"…But whoever would be great among you must be your servant, and whoever would be first among you must be your slave, even as the Son of Man came not to be served but to serve, and to give His life as a ransom for many." Matthew 20:26-28

All in a Day

Some days are rough;
Some days are great.
But every day I live to see
I truly appreciate.
For God has been gracious;
His mercies are new each day.
Whatever I am in need of
He faithfully sends my way.
To God be all the glory
For the things He has done;
From the rising to the setting
Of His magnificent sun.

"But as for me, I would seek God, and bring my problem before Him. Who does great things, and unsearchable, marvelous things without number. He gives rain on the earth, and sends waters on the fields. He sets on high those who are lowly, and those who mourn are lifted to safety." Job 5:8-11

My New Red Coat

Today I wore my new red coat
As pleased as I could be,
So thankful when Rev. Jacqua left,
She thought to give it to me.
Some time ago, I talked to God
About my aging attire.
I prayed that He would spice it up,
And now my closet's on fire!
I find it amazing how God will touch
The heart of another to share
With others who need a little help
In a way without putting on airs.
Such kindness I could never forget,
And truly I long for the day
When I am able to bless someone
In the same unselfish way.

"How abundant are the good things that You have stored up for those who fear You, which You bestow in the sight of all, on those who take refuge in You." Psalm 31:19

Into the Deep

Cast your net on the right side;
Launch out into the deep;
For therein dwells a catch
You will be delighted to keep.
For when God gives a command,
It is always for your good.
Even when His logic
Is not fully understood.
You need not know the reason,
It is yours to simply obey
And get ready for the blessing
He will joyfully send your way.

"When He had stopped speaking, He said to Simon, "Launch out into the deep and let down your nets for a catch." But Simon answered and said to Him, "Master, we have toiled all night and caught nothing; nevertheless at Your word I will let down the net." And when they had done this, they caught a great number of fish, and their net was breaking." Luke 5:4-6

Moving Day

Some things old, some things new,
Nothing borrowed, a few things blue;
So many things in one little house
For movers to pack, with nary a grouse.
They moved swiftly throughout the place
To finish their work at a diligent pace.
Always pleasant with each request
And quite determined to do their best.
In no time flat, they had a full load,
Collected their pay, and drove down the road.
I truly will miss spending time there,
Chatting with Ms. Jacqua about life's cares
And getting advice on how to cope
While remaining positive and full of hope.
I pray her ministry in Dallas goes well
As her story of faith she continues to tell
To help other women grow strong in the Lord
By receiving the peace only He can afford.

"And He Himself gave some to be apostles, some prophets, some evangelists, and some pastors and teachers, for the equipping of the saints for the work of ministry, for the edifying of the body of Christ." Ephesians 4:11-12

God Is There

When trouble comes around
Much more than you can bear,
Remember you can carry
Everything to God in prayer.
His ears are ever listening
To hear your faintest cry,
And if you call on Him,
He will not pass you by.

"Then they cried out to the LORD in their trouble, and He saved them out of their distresses. He brought them out of darkness and the shadow of death, and broke their bands asunder. Oh that men would praise the LORD for His goodness, and for His wonderful works to the children of men!" Psalm 107:13-15

Remember Not to Forget

Sometimes we need to remember
What we would like to forget:
The reckless moments in life,
That brought us much regret.
The times when we listened
And followed imprudent voices
That led us down a twisted path,
Making all the wrong choices,
Causing us to lament
As we languished in great pain,
Seeking the LORD for mercy
To remove each guilty stain.
Oh yes, we must remember,
So we dare not forget,
Lest we become ensnared again
To relive the same regret.

"Stand fast therefore in the liberty by which Christ has made us free, and do not be entangled again with a yoke of bondage." Galatians 5:1

Listen

When experience is teaching,
Embrace the One who is reaching
Out to save and bring you hope,
So you can learn how to cope
With the issues experienced in this life
That cause you pain and lead to strife.
Do not play the role of a "know-it-all;"
This sets the stage for a great big fall.
We all need help every now and then
To be loosed from the grip of death and sin,
For the Devil is lurking and he plays rough.
His burdens are heavy and his yoke is tough.
He lies in wait for the chance to deceive
And swoops in fast when you fail to believe
In the love and compassion God has for you
And the help in place for your rescue.

"The ear that listens to life-giving correction dwells among the wise. Those who refuse discipline despise themselves, but those who listen to correction gain understanding." Proverbs 15:31-32

Doing My Best

Before you know it, the day is gone,
With so little time to call your own.
You plan your work and work your plan
To carve a niche as best you can,
Hoping and praying along the way
You are able to brighten someone's day.
Perhaps in word or maybe in deed,
Your actions prove to meet a need.
For the life you live should not be in vain,
Nor should you strive for selfish gain.
Instead, be conscious of others you meet,
Even if that means giving up your seat;
For living is really not all about you,
But more about the good you can do.

"If your gift is serving, then serve; if it is teaching, then teach; if it is encouraging others, then encourage them; if it is giving, then give generously; if it is to lead, do it diligently; if it is to show mercy, do it cheerfully. Love must be sincere. Hate what is evil; cling to what is good. Be devoted to one another in love. Honor one another above yourselves." Romans 12:7-10

Meekness

Meekness is an attitude
Necessary to possess
If the earth you want to inherit
And all of its goodness.
Meekness helps you defer to others
When you want to have your own way;
It cloaks you in humility
And shows you how to obey.
Meekness draws its strength from God
To calm each restless soul;
It teaches you to have self-restraint,
So pride does not take control.

"Remind the believers to be subject to rulers and authorities, to obey them, to be ready to do good, to speak no evil about anyone, to live in peace, and to be gentle, showing all meekness unto all men." Titus 3:1-2

Oversight

The ones you overlooked
May have been the homely sort,
The type you would consider
Only as a last resort.

Their looks were just too average,
Their wardrobe rather bleak,
But you were too proud to be humble
And much too strong to be meek.

As time goes by so swiftly,
You find yourself driven to think
How God with a peculiar humor
Will knowingly give you a wink.

Your beauty ever fading,
For it was mostly skin deep,
In that moment of reflection
Has prompted you to weep;

For the one you once rejected
Has now become quite a prize.
No use crying over what could have been,
So dry your weeping eyes.

If only you had been wiser,
You would have been able to see
The potential in who was before you,
But in ignorance you set them free.

Now many years have slipped away.
You find yourself alone.
Resist the urge to continuously lament,
And come out of the "Twilight Zone!"

For God has not forgotten you;
He has a purpose in mind,
And when you choose to delight in Him,
Unspeakable joy you will find!

To some who were confident of their own righteousness and looked down on everyone else, Jesus told this parable: "Two men went up to the temple to pray, one a Pharisee and the other a tax collector. The Pharisee stood by himself and prayed: 'God, I thank you that I am not like other people: robbers, evildoers, adulterers, or even like this tax collector. I fast twice a week and give a tenth of all I get.' "But the tax collector stood at a distance. He would not even look up to heaven, but beat his breast and said, 'God, have mercy on me, a sinner.' "I tell you that this man, rather than the other, went home justified before God. For all those who exalt themselves will be humbled, and those who humble themselves will be exalted." Luke 18:9-14

Control

Take hold of the reins that control your life
By ridding yourself of bitterness and strife;
Let love abound when others hate;
What God commands do not debate.
Be controlled by His will and not your own
To avoid indulging what the flesh condones.
Remember through Christ you have the strength
To endure when testing is at great length;
Be patient and kind to everyone you meet
And remind them that victory overcomes defeat!

"Grace and peace be multiplied unto you through the knowledge of God and of Jesus our Lord. By His divine power the Lord has given to us all things that pertain to life and godliness through the knowledge of Him who has called us by His own glory and excellence, by which He has given to us exceedingly great and precious promises, so that through these things you might become partakers of the divine nature and escape the corruption that is in the world through lust. For this reason make every effort to add to your faith virtue; and to virtue knowledge; and to knowledge temperance; and to temperance patience; and to patience godliness; and to godliness brotherly kindness; and to brotherly kindness love." 2 Peter 1:2-7

Changed

I forgive myself,
I love myself,
I give myself a break;
For Jesus died
Upon the cross
To pay for my mistakes.
No more guilt,
No more shame,
No more feeling bad;
Since Jesus loved
And sacrificed,
I have no need to be sad.
Now I am free,
No longer bound,
My life has been made new.
With God on my side
I am truly blessed.
There is nothing I cannot do.

"Therefore, from now on, we regard no one according to the flesh. Even though we have known Christ according to the flesh, yet now we know Him thus no longer. Therefore, if anyone is in Christ, he is a new creation; old things have passed away; behold, all things have become new. Now all things are of God, who has reconciled us to Himself through Jesus Christ, and has given us the ministry of reconciliation, that is, that God was in Christ reconciling the world to Himself, not imputing their trespasses to them, and has committed to us the word of reconciliation."
2 Corinthians 5:16-19

Righteousness and Works

Hear ye! Hear ye!
All you worker bees!

Your righteousness is not based on works,
Although they have a few little perks.
For people will certainly know your name
And any associated claim to fame:

"I was on the planning committee
For the Women's Day affair.
Is my name on the program? Do you see it?
Oh, yes! It's listed right there!"

"Well, I led Bible study
Three weeks in a row!
They learn *so* much more from me.
Just thought I'd let you know."

"That's nothing because I directed the choir
And sang my favorite song.
My *performance* was absolutely *flawless*,
But *their* backup was just all wrong!"

"So! I work in the kitchen!
Isn't that worth honorable mention?
Whenever there is a program
And everyone wants to eat,
I arrange all of the dishes,
And that includes carving the meat!"

"Well, now, you all have nothing on me,
Because I'm on the Board of Trustees.
I hear what the pastor says,
But sometimes, I do as I please!"

"Wait a minute! Come over here!
Who's that sitting over there?"
"I think that's Sister Mary
Whispering her *same* old prayer."

"Lord, make me a vessel,
Willing to be used by Thee;
May you get all of the glory,
And none go unto me."

The moral of this story
By now you have figured out:
While works are to help the church function,
They are not what righteousness is about.

For it is only through salvation
Found in the Lord Jesus Christ
Are we able to be made righteous
And receive eternal life.

"But when the kindness and the love of God our Savior toward man appeared, not by works of righteousness which we have done, but according to His mercy He saved us, through the washing of regeneration and renewing of the Holy Spirit, whom He poured out on us abundantly through Jesus Christ our Savior, that having been justified by His grace we should become heirs according to the hope of eternal life." Titus 3:4-7

Tribute

This poem was written as a tribute to my friend and mentor, Rev. Jacqua. What a blessing it is when God places someone in your life to remind you He has not forgotten about you, that your life has value, and He has a plan to maximize your potential as you learn to follow Him. I am grateful for what I have learned and excited about how God will use me to sow into other people's lives to help them understand the same.

—Marcia

What you have done for me
I will try to explain:
You have prompted me to think
By stimulating my brain;
You have awakened the vision
I once dreamed could be;
You have spoken to potential
Dormant inside of me;
You have given beyond expectation
To exceed material need;
You have helped me summon the courage
To believe I could succeed;
You have opened up a door
Closed a long time ago;
You have introduced a woman
I am now delighted to know.
All these things, on your own,
I know you could not do,
But as I watched you glorify God,
I could see Him working through you!

"I pray that God would grant you, according to the riches of His glory, to be strengthened with might through His Spirit in the inner man, that Christ may dwell in your hearts through faith; that you, being rooted and grounded in love, may be able to comprehend with all the saints what is the width and length and depth and height — to know the love of Christ which passes knowledge; that you may be filled with all the fullness of God." Ephesians 3:16-19

Holding on to Hope

As I look around each day,
I see so many go astray.
Hear God's warning, please take heed,
Turn away from wicked deeds.
My sister, my brother, come to Christ!
Let Him give you a brand new life.
Trust Him with your heart and soul,
And He will gladly make you whole.
Receive His grace to help you grow;
Wash you clean and white as snow.
Read God's word and learn His way.
Let salvation come today.

"Repent therefore and be converted, that your sins may be blotted out, so that times of refreshing may come from the presence of the Lord." Acts 3:19

Grief

There is no time limit on grief,
So it is okay to cry.
When those you love pass away,
It is hard to say good-bye.
Eventually, your tears will cease
As you strive to carry on,
But still it hurts to think about
The fact that they are gone.
You wish you had just one more chance
To tell them how you feel,
To share another hearty laugh,
Or cook their favorite meal.
Although you know this cannot be,
There is no harm in wishing;
To have more than a memory
Of those you have been missing.

"And God will wipe away every tear from their eyes; there shall be no more death, nor sorrow, nor crying. There shall be no more pain, for the former things have passed away." Revelation 21:4

Just My Imagination

When the day is long and I am not feeling my best,
I long to find a place of rest;
Just get away and sit a spell;
Perhaps check into a luxury hotel
Someplace near a pristine beach,
Where clear blue waters are within arm's reach.
As I lean back in my posh lounge chair,
I toss away frustration and care,
And dream about how it would be
If lavish living was my reality.
Would that make me happy or content?
Or would I fret over the money I had spent?
But if I am rich, should that even matter?
I wake up to an hors d'oeuvre–filled platter,
Next to a refreshing, tropical drink.
I pick it up, take a sip, and I begin to think;
How nice it would be to live this way
And be at my leisure every day,
Doing exactly what I please
And having my mind totally at ease.
Alas, this day is not yet here,
But in my imagination, it is ever so clear!

"Behold, I am the Lord, the God of all flesh. Is there anything too hard for Me?" Jeremiah 32:27

Seek ME; Find ME

The one who wants ME
Will seek ME and find ME,
For I AM not hidden at all.
I AM not like the others
Who broke your heart
And failed to return your call.

I have waited so patiently
For you to reach out
To make ME your very own,
But I will not push
Or force myself,
If you tell ME to leave you alone.

I have watched you fall
And get back up,
Then have seen you turn around
To travel the same
Destructive path
That leaves you hurt and bound.

When you grow weary
Of doing this wrong,
Let ME show you how to love right,
So you can experience
A pure relationship
That will turn your darkness to light.

"Then you will call upon Me and go and pray to Me, and I will listen to you. And you will seek Me and find Me, when you search for Me with all your heart." Jeremiah 29:12-13

A Voice in the Valley

In the valley of decision,
I have to make a choice.
Dear Lord, speak loud and clear,
So I can hear Your voice
And know without a doubt
What I am called to do
And how I am to serve
That will best glorify You.
I know You have a purpose
For the gifts You have placed in me.
Please show me how to use them
And where I am meant to be,
For in this ordained season,
I dare not choose wrong.
So Lord, I ask for clarity
And courage to be strong!

"I will instruct you (says the Lord) and guide you along the best pathway for your life; I will advise you and watch your progress." Psalm 32:8

Oh Valentine, So True

As Valentine's Day approaches, some get the shakes.
But calm down now, for goodness sakes.
Is there anything wrong with not having a date?
Is this a requirement to participate?
With all of the excitement as love comes to call,
There is a love that can be shared by all:
The love of the Father, Son, and Holy Ghost;
Truly the Ones who love you the most!
Much better than candy, flowers, or a jewel
That make some covet and others drool.
For certain there are people who will go without,
But do not be angry and do not pout.
Just focus on the love These Three have for you,
And this will eliminate the urge to feel blue.
The Father loved you so that He gave His only Son;
The Son loved you so that He chose to be the One
Who redeemed your soul by laying down His life
To free you from sin that leads to strife.
Now if that is not enough to make you swoon,
What I share next should send you over the moon!
When the Son reunited with the Father above,
He sent you a Comforter to express His love,
And this is the Holy Ghost, Spirit of the Living God.
So if you are single, you need not feel odd,
For the Comforter, your helper, counselor, and friend
Will stick like glue to the very end.
Hence, rest assured when Cupid aims his bow,
This Triune love is the best you could ever know!

"For God so loved the world that He gave His only begotten Son, that whoever believes in Him should not perish but have everlasting life. For God did not send His Son into the world to condemn the world, but that the world through Him might be saved." John 3:16-17

Live for Today

Live for today, as tomorrow is yet to be;
Yesterday is gone, no longer a mystery.
We cannot change the past by dwelling in remorse
Or by wishing we had taken an alternate course.
Make each day better by learning from the past;
Misfortune and mayhem does not have to last.
There is nothing we can do to make the day last longer.
Tomorrow is not a prize if we are braver or stronger.
Plan for the future and strive with all to do well,
By answering the call to help others excel.
For surely God is pleased when we love one another.
What good is our gain, if we fail to lift our brother?
The value of each day we cannot truly measure,
Yet each one we are given is a gift to treasure.

"This is the day the Lord has made; we will rejoice and be glad in it." Psalm 118:24
"Do not boast about tomorrow, for you do not know what a day may bring forth." Proverbs 27:1

Sanctuary

Flying on the wings of love
To heights that are unknown,
Fastened in the Master's arms,
I'm in the safety zone.
There no foe can destroy me;
No evil will come nigh.
By trusting and obeying God,
I know my path He'll guide.
He'll lead me to a hilltop
To see where my help comes from.
He'll be a tent to cover
And shield me from the storm.
He'll be the bread that feeds me,
My water when I thirst.
He'll be my strength to press on
When I'm feeling my worst.
This safety I have known so long
Gives great comfort to me.
It protects me from a world of harm—
No better place to be.

"But no weapon that is formed against you shall prosper, and every tongue that shall rise against you in judgment you shall show to be in the wrong. This [peace, righteousness, security, triumph over opposition] is the heritage of the servants of the Lord [those in whom the ideal Servant of the Lord is reproduced]; this is the righteousness or the vindication which they obtain from Me [this is that which I impart to them as their justification], says the Lord." Isaiah 54:17

Just in Time

When God smiles at me,
It feels so good!
In that one moment,
I feel totally understood!
All of the days, months, and years,
Which seem to go rolling by,
Where I have found myself questioning
And wondering why
Things take so long,
And when they will change.
I suppose this was normal,
Even though I felt strange.
But I am encouraged,
And I have no doubt
Everything God has for me
Will soon come about!

"But blessed is the one who trusts in the Lord, whose confidence is in Him. They will be like a tree planted by the water that sends out its roots by the stream. It does not fear when heat comes; its leaves are always green. It has no worries in a year of drought and never fails to bear fruit." Jeremiah 17:7-8

Dear Son

Who you are and what you will be
Is not always easy for the eye to see,
But the God who created you knew so much more than me.

He knew your struggles; He knew your pain.
But He also knew the strength you would gain
In spite of almost going insane.

Insane? Yes! When the path is not clear
And you wrestle with fear,
It is hard to sense the Savior is near.

But He is, and He cares,
And He is very aware,
So do not doubt or despair.

God has a plan,
And it will not be hindered by man
When you do the best you can.

Oh, I remember when you thought you knew it all
And seldom felt the need to call
Because you were too busy having a ball,

But now I see you fully grown,
Working your way out of that zone
To find a place to call your own.

Albeit your breakthrough is not in sight,
Be assured it will come when you walk in God's light
And trust Him to make everything all right!

"Even to your old age and gray hairs I am He, I am He who will sustain you. I have made you and I will carry you; I will sustain you and I will rescue you." Isaiah 46:4

Wake Up

Lord, who will stand in the gap
While the world takes a nap;
Pushing snooze as the alarm clock rings,
Deceived by visions of profane things;
Believing that "time is on our side,"
No sense of urgency to abide
In Your Word, according to Your will;
Naively thinking, it's no big deal
To live holy and walk upright,
Be it morning, noon, or night.
Hold back Your wrath, O Lord, we pray.
Send destruction far away.
Call us Lord, unplug our ears,
Lest we drown in a pool of tears.

"So I sought for a man among them who would make a wall, and stand in the gap before Me on behalf of the land, that I should not destroy it; but I found no one. Therefore I have poured out My indignation on them; I have consumed them with the fire of My wrath; and I have recompensed their deeds on their own heads," says the Lord God. "Ezekiel 22:30-31
" If My people, who are called by My name shall humble themselves, and pray, and seek My face, and turn from their wicked ways; then will I hear from heaven, and will forgive their sin, and will heal their land."
2 Chronicles 7:14

GOD

Oh God!
Great God!
Mighty God!
Merciful God!

Alpha and Omega!
The "I AM That I AM!"
Omnipotent creator!
Father of the Lamb!

God of salvation,
God of grace,
God of deliverance,
Unveil my face!

Fill me!
Transform me!
Prepare me!
Send me!
Give me ears to hear,
A resolve to obey.
When I open my mouth,
Give me what to say!

As Your gospel is spread throughout,
May Your glory fill the earth,
Restoring hope to all mankind
As they receive their second birth!

For there is none like You,
The One who loves us all.
You hasten to perform Your word
Whenever we dare to call!

"Nevertheless when one turns to the Lord, the veil is taken away. Now the Lord is the Spirit; and where the Spirit of the Lord is, there is liberty. And we all, with unveiled face, beholding the glory of the Lord, are being transformed into the same image from glory to glory, just as by the Spirit of the Lord." 2 Corinthians 3:16-18

Get Over It

Brooding over your past
And what you did not do
Will hinder your ability
To see what is good in you.
So give yourself a break
The next time you recall
A moment you fell short
Or failed to give your all
And pray for understanding
To know which way is right,
So you can choose well
To ensure your future is bright.

"Remember not the former things, neither consider the things of old. Behold, I will do a new thing; now it shall spring forth; shall you not know it? I will even make a way in the wilderness, and rivers in the desert." Isaiah 43:18-19

Faith

Not what is,
But what will be.
Not based on sight,
But what we believe.
God will do
In the right season.
Why He waits
May seem beyond reason.
But we should know
God is infinitely wise.
There is simply no need
To have tears in our eyes.
For God is never late,
And He is not slow.
He has a purpose
We have yet to know.
Hence, be not dismayed
When facing a test.
Keep trusting in God,
For He knows best!

"Now faith is the assurance (the confirmation, the title deed) of the things [we] hope for, being the proof of things [we] do not see and the conviction of their reality [faith perceiving as real fact what is not revealed to the senses]." Hebrews 11:1

In His Hands

In His Hands,
My image is engraved;
In His Hands,
From danger I am saved;
In His Hands,
I have shelter from the storm;
In His Hands,
He keeps me safe and warm;
In His Hands,
All my need is met;
In His Hands,
I live without regret;
In His Hands,
My future looks bright;
In His Hands,
He makes everything all right!

"Can a woman forget her nursing child, and not have compassion on the son of her womb? Even these may forget, yet I will not forget you. Behold, I have engraved you on the palms of my hands; your walls are continually before me. Your sons shall make haste; your destroyers and those who laid you waste shall go away from you. Lift up your eyes, look around and see; all these gather together and come to you. As I live, says the Lord, you shall surely clothe yourselves with them all as an ornament, and bind them on you as a bride does." Isaiah 49:15-18

Religion, Relationship, and Church

Religion, Relationship, and Church—
Which one is important for you?
I have found each to add value
To what we think and do.

Good religion shows due diligence
To practice a task every day.
It can often appear to be genuine
When we know just what to say.

It is possible to form a relationship
Apart from going to church,
But if we choose to live without it,
We will soon find ourselves in a lurch.

For when God appoints the pastor of a church,
He anoints him oh so well.
He sends down manna from heaven,
Filled with spiritual truths to tell.

Now before we judge the pastor
And question credentials and skill,
We should be sure our standard of living
Lines up with the Father's will.

We can all read and quote scriptures
And use them to prove a point,
Whether sitting inside the church house
Or toe tapping at the local juke joint.

For certain, we all have the liberty
To devise and choose our own plan.
But without sound wisdom from God,
It is subject to the defects of man.

Although we enjoy doing things our way,
It is always best to adhere
To instruction found in the Bible
And hold God's principles dear.

To develop the best relationship
With the Father, Son, and Holy Ghost,
We must work to develop all three,
For then we will grow the most!

"Till I come, give attention to reading, to exhortation, to doctrine. Do not neglect the gift that is in you, which was given to you by prophecy with the laying on of the hands of the eldership. Meditate on these things; give yourself entirely to them, that your progress may be evident to all." 1 Timothy 4:13-15

God Is

God is Able,
Even when we believe He is not;
God is Faithful,
Even when we think He forgot;
God is Punctual,
Even when we consider Him late;
God is Available,
Even when we hesitate;
God is Genuine,
Even when we are fake;
God is Merciful,
Even when we make a mistake;
God is Patient,
Even when we cannot make up our minds;
God is Compassionate,
Even when we are less than kind.
God is All
We could ever truly need;
When we emulate Him,
We are destined to succeed!

"Therefore be imitators of God, as beloved children; and walk in love, just as Christ also loved you and gave Himself up for us, an offering and a sacrifice to God as a fragrant aroma." Ephesians 5:1-2

Detours

When we fail to listen for God's voice,
We tend to make the wrong choice.
Being bound and determined to have it our way
Typically leads to unwanted delay
In receiving all God has in store
When we walk through His open door
To find the treasure He has put aside
For those who willingly choose to abide
In His presence both day and night,
And decide, on purpose, to walk in the light;
Forsaking the flesh to obtain this prize
Would truly be considered wise.

*"Now it shall come to pass, if you diligently obey the voice of the Lord your God, to observe carefully all His commandments which I command you today, that the Lord your God will set you high above all nations of the earth....The Lord will open to you His good treasure, the heavens, to give the rain to your land in its season, and to bless all the work of your hand. You shall lend to many nations, but you shall not borrow. And the Lord will make you the head and not the tail; you shall be above only, and not be beneath, if you heed the commandments of the Lord your God, which I command you today, and are careful to observe them. So you shall not turn aside from any of the words which I command you this day, to the right or the left, to go after other gods to serve them."
Deuteronomy 28:1; 12-14*

Remembering Mama

I remember when Mama
Used to take us to the store.
We did not drive a car,
But the walk was never a bore.
Together we would stroll
Down the street, hand in hand,
Excited by the thought
Of what our Mama had planned.
Not only would she purchase
The items on her list,
But also thought to buy
A treat we could not resist.
Anticipation would mount
As we rounded the corner below.
Our destination in view,
We did not have far to go!
This tiny little market
Was not much to behold,
But for those who had a need,
It was priceless as pure gold.
Sometimes we ran short on money,
But still we were able to buy;
With the promise to pay later,
We could partake of their supply.
Upon returning home,
Mama prepared to cook.
There were lots of tasty dishes
In her recipe book.
One item Mama would make
That made our walk worthwhile;
She called them "Cocoa Indians."
Even the memory makes me smile.

I can still recall the smell
Of cocoa wafting through the air;
It reminds me of Mama's love
And how she has never failed to care.

"Strength and dignity are her clothing, and she laughs at the time to come. She opens her mouth with wisdom, and the teaching of kindness is on her tongue. She looks well to the ways of her household and does not eat the bread of idleness." Proverbs 31:25-27

Transition

We are all a work in progress,
Not quite where we should be.
As we strive to please the Lord,
He will open our eyes to see
The route we are to take
In accordance to His plan
To become a faithful servant,
And live the best we can.

"For am I now seeking the approval of man, or of God? Or am I trying to please man? If I were still trying to please man, I would not be a servant of Christ." Galatians 1:10

All You Need

To satisfy our cravings
And quench our every thirst,
Before we choose wrong,
We must seek the LORD first!

He has a full supply
And never shall run out.
When we delight in Him,
We will never experience drought!

He has sent the invitation
For all to come and dine,
To partake in the richest of fare
That will surely taste divine!

You will have no need of money;
This affair is totally free.
Our Savior lovingly paid the cost
When He died on Calvary!

"Come, all you who are thirsty, come to the waters; and you who have no money, come, buy and eat! Come; buy wine and milk without money and without cost. Why spend money on what is not bread, and your labor on what does not satisfy? Listen, listen to me, and eat what is good and you will delight in the richest of fare. Give ear and come to me; listen, that you may live. I will make an everlasting covenant with you, even the sure mercies of David." Isaiah 55:1-3

From Heaven to Earth

"When Heaven Speaks,"
Give ear to pay attention,
To avoid the need of a cure
By subscribing to prevention.
Time is swiftly approaching
When trouble is going to cease,
And those who trust in the Lord
Will experience glorious peace.
For surely someone is praying,
Beseeching the Father above,
To pour out tender mercies
And surround us with His love.
Oh Lord, speak to our minds
And tell us what to do,
So we may be found worthy
To live in Heaven with You!

"Indeed, let no one who waits on You be ashamed; let those be ashamed who deal treacherously without cause. Show me Your ways, O Lord; teach me Your paths. Lead me in Your truth and teach me, for You are the God of my salvation; on You I wait all the day." Psalm 25:3-5

Impressions

We came into this world
Weak and helpless;
Unable to fend for ourselves;
Naked and unashamed;
A blank slate, so to speak.
Who will write on us?
What will they say?
How will they shape us?
What will we do
With the life we have been given?
Will we pen a celebrated novel?
Will we champion an epic movement?
Will we discover a much needed cure?
Will we mesmerize and amaze
As we pontificate from the alter
About life,
About reward and punishment,
About right from wrong,
About good and evil,
About heaven or hell?
And who will go?
Who dares to judge?
Who is worthy?
Worthy is the Lamb
In Whom we have our being
And purpose for living.

"And He made from one man every nation of mankind to live on all the face of the earth, having determined allotted periods and the boundaries

of their dwelling place, that they should seek God, in the hope that they might feel their way toward Him and find Him. Yet He is actually not far from each one of us, for 'In Him we live and move and have our being'; as even some of your own poets have said, 'For we are indeed His offspring.'" Acts 17:26-28

In His Image

A God-made man,
Is on a mission;
No time to be idle
Or stray from position.
He has no boot straps
To pull up on,
But rather he hastens
Before God's throne,
Studying the Word
Both day and night
To know the truth
And walk upright,
Never leaning
Unto his own way,
But freely choosing
To trust and obey.

"But we all, with unveiled face, beholding as in a mirror the glory of the Lord, are being transformed into the same image from glory to glory, just as by the Spirit of the Lord." 2 Corinthians 3:18

Soul Rage

> *Expect the unexpected because just when you think it won't happen to you, it does. That moment when life sucker punches you in the gut and momentarily takes your breath away, causing you to scream deep down inside as you fight back tears so no one else can see how deeply grieved you are. In that moment, as you fight for air and try not to hate, the enemy laughs and begins to boast to his demonic clan that he's won; that you'll never recover from this experience. Not so! It is in this moment when we must truly cast every care on the LORD and trust Him to care for us, vindicate us, and appropriately deal with those who have grievously vexed our souls. The devil is a LIE! He was defeated at Calvary when my Savior and LORD, Jesus Christ, the Messiah hung, bled, and died for the remission of my sins and the sins of the whole world! To give the gift of salvation for whosoever will call upon the name of the LORD. If you haven't called Him, today is the day; tomorrow is NOT guaranteed.*
>
> *—Marcia*

Sometimes, there are no words
To express what is in the heart.
When the unexpected comes
And rips your soul apart!
It is truly in this moment
That faith *must* kick in
To prevent us from thinking
Evil that leads to sin.
Do not be dismayed;
Resist the urge to doubt,
For the Father knows just how
To straighten everything out.
He is the balm to heal
Every hurt and pain,
To restore the wounded spirit,
So we can breathe again.

"Blessed be the God and Father of our Lord Jesus Christ, the Father of mercies and God of all comfort, who comforts us in all our tribulation, that we may be able to comfort those who are in any trouble, with the comfort with which we ourselves are comforted by God." 2 Corinthians 1:3-4

Keep On Keeping Me

Lord, keep me humble
And please keep me pure.
For every problem I face
Give me strength to endure.
Provide a way of escape
When temptation draws near.
Cover me with Your mercy
And cast away all fear.
Order each step I take,
So I can walk upright
To live a life that is pleasing
And holy in Your sight.

"In this you greatly rejoice, though now for a little while, if need be, you have been grieved by various trials, that the genuineness of your faith, being much more precious than gold that perishes, though it is tested by fire, may be found to praise, honor, and glory at the revelation of Jesus Christ." 1 Peter 1:6-7

The Real Deal

Heaven is for real,
But so is Hell.
What will happen there,
No one wants to tell.

No mercy to be found,
Not even an ounce.
Only misery and demons
Eager to pounce!

No parties in Hell,
No hint of paradise,
No chilling with the homies.
Nothing about it will be nice.

Perhaps it would be easy
To sit passively by
And watch others perish
Without batting an eye,

But this is not what
We are called to do.
God did not save us
To merely warm a pew.

We must share the truth,
So others can go free,
By surrendering to Christ
To live in victory.

"But in accordance with your hardness and your impenitent heart you are treasuring up for yourself wrath in the day of wrath and revelation of the righteous judgment of God, who 'will render to each one according to his deeds': eternal life to those who by patient continuance in doing good seek for glory, honor, and immortality; but to those who are self-seeking and do not obey the truth, but obey unrighteousness—indignation and wrath." Romans 2:5-8

Night Lights

On my way home tonight
I beheld a sable sky.
Lightning flashed and soared
As it tangoed with the clouds.
The moon and stars glowed dimly
Beneath a mysterious hue.
A gentle breeze stirred the air,
Blowing a delicate mist through my window;
Kissing my face.
I just wanted to keep driving
To behold this majestic exhibit
Of the elements and nature at play!

"Hearken unto this, O Job: stand still, and consider the wondrous works of God. Do you know when God dispatched them, and caused the light of his cloud to shine? Do you know the balancing of the clouds, the wondrous works of Him which is perfect in knowledge?" Job 37:14-16

A Good Return

If you are tired of reaping
The same old crop,
Take the Sword of the Spirit
And chop, chop, chop!
Cut out the weed of bitterness
That springs from the root of scorn;
Then plow up every fear and doubt
That has delivered your dreams stillborn.
Next, fertilize your soil
With a mix of peace, joy, and love,
And pray for mercy to fall
Like rain from heaven above.
Now as the Son shines bright,
Be patient, watch, and pray,
And soon your harvest will come
In a marvelous array,
Generating new life,
Bearing fruit for all to see,
Yielding a glorious season
Of abundant prosperity.

"I am the true vine, and My Father is the vinedresser. Every branch in Me that does not bear fruit He takes away; and every branch that bears fruit He prunes, that it may bear more fruit. You are already clean because of the word which I have spoken to you. Abide in Me, and I in you. As the branch cannot bear fruit of itself, unless it abides in the vine, neither can you, unless you abide in Me. "I am the vine, you are the branches. He who abides in Me, and I in him, bears much fruit; for without Me you can do nothing." John 15:1-5

Every Step of the Way

Father, show us your glory
And teach us what to say;
Then order our steps
As we go about each day.
When trials come,
And they will,
Help us to trust You
And learn to be still,
Knowing by faith
You already have a plan
To transform our lives
Without the sanction of man.
For You know our beginning,
As well as our end.
When others fall away,
On You we can depend
To keep us in a dry place.
Or when everything is well,
An ever-present strength,
To ensure we prevail!

"He that overcomes will I make a pillar in the temple of My God, and he shall go no more out: and I will write upon him the name of My God, and the name of the city of My God, which is new Jerusalem, which comes down out of heaven from My God: and I will write upon him My new name. He that has an ear, let him hear what the Spirit says unto the churches." Revelation 3:12-13

My Source, My All

Calling forth a "Right Now Praise"
For every blessing from God,
Even when the circumstances
Leave me feeling a little odd;
Wondering what will happen
And wondering what to do,
But somehow resting assured
My God will see me through.
He knows all the particulars
Of each dilemma I will face;
Hence, I trust Him to supply
A sufficient amount of grace
To keep me in the valley
When times are somewhat lean,
Or standing on the mountain top
To behold abundance never seen.
Yes, My God is amazing!
He has never forsaken me!
My soul is filled with hope
As I anticipate victory.

"Cause me to hear Your lovingkindness in the morning, for in You do I trust; cause me to know the way in which I should walk, for I lift up my soul to You. Deliver me, O LORD, from my enemies; I flee unto You to hide me. Teach me to do Your will; for You are my God: Your Spirit is good; lead me into the land of uprightness." Psalm 143:8-10

Going Forward

I may not be able to change
The things that I have done,
But I can look unto the East
And watch for the rising sun,
Peering over the horizon
To shatter my darkest night,
While offering assurance
Everything will be alright.
As I cry out for mercy,
LORD, endow me with grace,
So I will have sufficient strength
To run this Christian race.
Purge me of unrighteousness
And draw me close to see
The abundant life awaiting
When I surrender all to Thee.

"O Lord, do not rebuke me in Your anger, nor chasten me in Your hot displeasure. Have mercy on me, O Lord, for I am weak; O Lord, heal me, for my bones are troubled. My soul also is greatly troubled; but You, O Lord, how long? Return, O Lord, deliver me! Oh, save me for Your mercies' sake!" Psalm 6:1-4

Praise Worthy

Rise up! Overcome!
Everybody rejoice!
Sing unto the Lord
With a loud voice:
Hosanna in the highest!
O bless His holy name!
Worship and adore Him.
Let all the saints proclaim
Worthy is our Lord.
Yes, so amazing is He;
Without His protective arm,
Just where would we be?
When persecution mounts
And trials dim our view,
I AM will be our strength
And come to our rescue.
Defeating every foe
That strives to make us fail,
Restoring hope and joy,
Ensuring we prevail.

"But You have saved us from our enemies, and have put to shame those who hated us. In God we boast all day long, and praise Your name forever. Selah" Psalm 44:7-8

Practice Makes Perfect

Pay attention choir!
Let's get this right,
So we can go home
And not be here all night.
Stop all that talking
In the fourth row.
I need you to listen,
Or I need you to go.
Don't mean to be short,
But we have a lot to do.
What time we leave
Greatly depends on you.

"Let the word of Christ dwell in you richly in all wisdom, teaching and admonishing one another in psalms and hymns and spiritual songs, singing with grace in your hearts to the Lord. And whatever you do in word or deed, do all in the name of the Lord Jesus, giving thanks to God the Father through Him." Colossians 3:16-17

Who You Gonna Call?

Who you gonna call
When times are rough,
When you feel like giving up
Cuz you've had enough?
Who you gonna call
When your friends are few,
When you're desperate for change
But don't know what to do?
Who you gonna call
When you've lost all hope,
When try as you might
You just can't cope?
The solution, though simple,
To some may be odd.
Cry out to Jesus Christ,
The begotten Son of God!
He can heal your broken body,
Refresh your wounded soul,
Save you from destruction,
Transform and make you whole.
As He did for Aeneas,
Paralyzed for eight years,
Confined to a bed of affliction,
No doubt infused with tears.
Then along comes Peter
To complete the task at hand.
With authority from on high,
This man was made to stand.
Praise God for every miracle
Recorded in His word
That brings reassurance
When deliverance is deferred.

"Now it came to pass, as Peter went through all parts of the country, that he also came down to the saints who dwelt in Lydda. There he found a certain man named Aeneas, who had been bedridden eight years and was paralyzed. And Peter said to him, 'Aeneas, Jesus the Christ heals you. Arise and make your bed.' Then he arose immediately." Acts 9:32-34

Nothing to Lose

Stop grieving over your past.
Acknowledge where you are today.
Trust God for a glorious future
In spite of what others say.
Sometimes what you want
Is just not meant to be.
Ask God for wisdom,
And He will help you see
The right path to follow
That leads to an open door;
If only you dare to enter
Can you experience more
Life in abundance,
Joy that is complete,
A strategy to win,
And never accept defeat.

"But the word is very near unto you, in your mouth and in your heart, that you may do it. See, I have set before you this today life and good, and death and evil, in that I command you this today to love the LORD your God, to walk in His ways, and to keep His commandments, and His statutes, and His judgments, that you may live and multiply: and the LORD your God shall bless you in the land which you go to possess." Deuteronomy 30:14-16

On Bended Knee

The battle we must fight
To defeat the enemy
Cannot be won with gun or sword
But rather on bended knee.
For when we pray unto the Lord
To shift the atmosphere,
He hearkens to our cries for help
And hastens to draw near:
Stepping down from heaven,
With a fierce consuming fire;
Delivering us from danger,
According to His desire;
Destroying every obstacle,
With quite an elaborate show.
See lightning flash and soar
As the earth trembles below.
Who else but the Lord
Could execute such a feat,
Conquering every foe,
So our victory is complete?

"The Lord lives! Blessed be my Rock! Let the God of my salvation be exalted. It is God who avenges me, and subdues the peoples under me; He delivers me from my enemies. You also lift me up above those who rise against me; You have delivered me from the violent man. Therefore I will give thanks to You, O Lord, among the Gentiles, and sing praises to Your name." Psalm 18:46-49

Faithful

When you open your eyes
To see another day,
Pause for a moment,
Give thanks, and pray
To the God who has carried you
All through the night
And allowed you to rise
With the morning light.
Cry out with assurance,
Knowing He will hear
The petitions of your heart
And hasten to draw near.
God finds no pleasure
In the wicked or boastful,
But the righteous have reason
To remain ever hopeful.
What God has promised
He is faithful to do.
Just put Him to the test
And watch Him come through.

"For You, O LORD, will bless the righteous; with favor You will surround him as with a shield." Psalm 5:12

From Wilderness to Wonder

Standing in the wilderness,
Weary from the view,
Crying out to God
To hasten our breakthrough.
Leading us to the land
He specifically designed
To manifest His goodness
And bring us peace of mind;
Delivering us from bondage
Created by fear and doubt
As we wrestled with the flesh,
Trying to figure things out;
Causing us to dwell
In a low place far too long,
Constantly reminded
Of everything gone wrong
Until we sought the Lord,
Author of our days;
Submitting to His will,
And careful to give Him praise
For the joy He has given us
And the new life we have found.
Let us magnify His holy name
As we stand on higher ground.

"The LORD our God spoke to us in Horeb, saying: 'You have dwelt long enough at this mountain. Turn you, and take your journey, and go to the mountains of the Amorites, and unto all the places near there, in the plain, in the hills, and in the lowland, and in the south, and by the sea side, to the land of the Canaanites, and unto Lebanon, unto the great river, the river Euphrates. Behold, I have set the land before you:

go in and possess the land which the LORD swore unto your fathers, Abraham, Isaac, and Jacob, to give unto them and to their seed after them." Deuteronomy 1:6-8

It's the Law

Ignorance of the law
Will offer no excuse.
Read the fine print
Or suffer its abuse.
Sign your name on the dotted line
In haste without apprehension.
Unwittingly, you lose the right
To defend your position!
When mistakes lead to enduring loss,
Causing you deep regret,
It will likely teach you a lesson
You will not soon forget.
However, do not despair
Or contemplate giving in.
With God Almighty on your side,
You still have potential to win!

"But we have this treasure in earthen vessels, that the excellence of the power may be of God and not of us. We are hard-pressed on every side, yet not crushed; we are perplexed, but not in despair; persecuted, but not forsaken; struck down, but not destroyed." 2 Corinthians 4:7-9

An Appointed Time

Complaining and whining,
I have done my share.
But whoever said
Life would be fair?
If we had our druthers,
We would always be on top,
But with nary a plan,
We end up as a flop.
No one likes to lose
Or get upset,
But along with the highs
We experience regret.
Though gusty winds blow
And rain must fall,
Take courage in knowing
God is there through it all.

"Though the fig tree may not blossom, nor fruit be on the vines; though the labor of the olive may fail, and the fields yield no food; though the flock may be cut off from the fold, and there be no herd in the stalls, yet I will rejoice in the Lord, I will joy in the God of my salvation. The Lord God is my strength; He will make my feet like deer's feet, and He will make me walk on my high hills." Habakkuk 3:17-19

Satisfied in HIM

Lord, in Your presence
Is everything we need.
Your Word is the bread of life
From which our souls feed.
Daily, You quench our thirst
From Your well of living waters,
Compelling us to become
Redeemed sons and daughters,
Freeing us from guilt
And the penalty of sin,
Filling us with Your Spirit,
Transforming us within,
To become new creations
Determined to live right,
Leading others out of darkness
Into Your marvelous light.

"And if you draw out your soul to the hungry, and satisfy the afflicted soul; then shall your light rise in the darkness, and your darkness be as the noon day: And the LORD shall guide you continually, and satisfy your soul in drought, and make fat your bones: and you shall be like a watered garden, and like a spring of water, whose waters fail not." Isaiah 58:10-11

Fine Tune

When we begin to grow
In the knowledge of the Lord,
Our previous carnal whims
Will strike a dissonant chord,
Opposing the righteous path
We now desire to follow
Instead of worthless pursuits
That left us broken and hollow.
Soon those we used to know
Will see there has been a change;
Some may believe it is good,
While others will find it strange.
Regardless of their view,
Continue to trust and obey
To gain peace that comes by faith
As we let God have His way.

"You therefore, beloved, seeing you know these things before; beware lest you also, being led away with the error of the wicked, fall from your own steadfastness. But grow in grace, and in the knowledge of our Lord and Savior Jesus Christ. To Him be glory both now and forever. Amen." 2 Peter 3:17-18

Higher Ground

When it seems your position
Has distanced you from the pack,
Keep marching towards your destiny
And refrain from looking back.
For what now lies behind
Can no longer hinder you
Or keep you from the work
Predestined for you to do.
For what the Lord allowed
Served to strengthen and condition,
Equipping you for the journey
To fulfill His glorious mission
Of reaching lost souls
Tortured by sin and strife,
By declaring salvation through Jesus
That leads to eternal life.

"Being then made free from sin, you became the servants of righteousness. For when you were the servants of sin, you were free from righteousness. What fruit had you then in those things of which you are now ashamed? For the end of those things is death. But now being made free from sin, and become servants to God, you have your fruit unto holiness, and the end everlasting life. For the wages of sin is death; but the gift of God is eternal life through Jesus Christ our Lord." Romans 6:18; 20-23

The Beautiful Gate

Day after day they carried me
To sit at the Beautiful Gate.
As I sat, I had nothing but time
To watch and contemplate
On the state of my condition
Of being lame since birth,
Feeling tired and dejected
While questioning my worth.
As the visibly whole paraded in,
Well attired and quite proud,
I remained outside the temple,
For the broken were not allowed.
As the time for prayer drew close,
Two men approached and walked by.
I solicited them for alms
And awaited their reply.
One spoke and said to look at them.
I complied without hesitation,
Expecting to receive
A monetary donation.
Much to my dismay,
They had no silver or gold.
What I was told to do next
Really struck me as bold:
"In the name of Jesus Christ of Nazareth,
Rise up and walk!"
He spoke with such authority,
I did not dare balk!
Taking me by the right hand,
He raised me to a standing position,
And immediately I gained strength,
Utterly changing my condition!

I could now enter the temple
Along with the other saints,
Walking, leaping, and praising God,
Full of joy and no complaints!
Oh bless the name of the Lord.
Draw nigh to His mercy seat.
In Him, find everything you need
To make soul and body complete.

"Then Peter said, 'Silver and gold I do not have, but what I do have I give you: In the name of Jesus Christ of Nazareth, rise up and walk.' And he took him by the right hand and lifted him up, and immediately his feet and ankle bones received strength. So he, leaping up, stood and walked and entered the temple with them— walking, leaping, and praising God." Acts 3:6-8

A New Direction

Looking back over wasted years
Can prompt the shedding of tears
When you think about time lost
And what each decision cost.
Whose fault is it anyway
When you encounter delay?
You can spend life blaming,
Or you can spend it aiming.
If you find a goal to aspire to,
You never know what you might do.
Though the best-laid plans can fail,
Persistence will help you prevail,
To become who God created you to be
As you forge ahead victoriously.

"Brethren, I do not count myself to have apprehended; but one thing I do, forgetting those things which are behind and reaching forward to those things which are ahead, I press toward the goal for the prize of the upward call of God in Christ Jesus." Philippians 3:13-14

A Family Affair

One big happy family,
Bound by a common strand;
Washed in the Blood of Jesus,
An extension of God's hand;
Sent to redeem lost mankind
And restore us to the place
Of fellowship with the Father,
Surrounded by His grace.
He teaches us how to love
And forgive our sisters and brothers
While exercising humility,
Showing mercy towards others.
For in the family of God
On any given day,
Those longing for acceptance
Should find it coming their way
To help them discover
Their role in God's plan;
To rescue the perishing,
Bringing hope and peace to man!

"Now, therefore, you are no longer strangers and foreigners, but fellow citizens with the saints and members of the household of God, having been built on the foundation of the apostles and prophets, Jesus Christ Himself being the chief cornerstone, in whom the whole building, being fitted together, grows into a holy temple in the Lord, in whom you also are being built together for a dwelling place of God in the Spirit." Ephesians 2:19-22

Vessels

When we are willing vessels,
God uses us to pour
Into the lives of others,
So they will trust Him more
And experience salvation
Freely given to all
When on the Name of Jesus
They are led to call.
We may not sound alike
Or use the same technique,
But we can all do something
To strengthen those who are weak.
For the Spirit abiding in us
Can transform anyone
Who humbly submits
To God's only begotten Son.

"As you know how we exhorted, and comforted, and charged every one of you, as a father does his own children, that you would walk worthy of God who calls you into His own kingdom and glory. For this reason we also thank God without ceasing, because when you received the word of God which you heard from us, you welcomed it not as the word of men, but as it is in truth, the word of God, which also effectively works in you who believe." 1 Thessalonians 2:11-13

Emotions

Feelings will change
With the shifting of the wind.
When emotions lead,
They are subject to offend.
What must I do?
Where should I go?
Who am I?
Does anybody know?
Frustrated? Bewildered?
You need not be.
Trust in the LORD,
Who helps the blind see
The error of their ways
And division in their hearts.
Be transformed today
By the love grace imparts!

"For if our heart condemns us, God is greater than our heart, and knows all things. Beloved, if our heart does not condemn us, we have confidence toward God." 1 John 3:20-21

Charlie

Today, I met Charlie.
He was worn and beaten from life.
From the looks of his appearance,
He had seen many years of strife.
When he first approached my car
To initiate a conversation,
I rolled the window down
With considerable reservation.
For I had seen many like him before
As I travel daily about town,
Standing on the side of the road,
Seeking alms and sorely cast down.
As he began to speak,
I braced for his request,
For I knew he wanted money,
Just like all the rest.
He asked for only one quarter.
Ironically, I had none.
He wanted to show me something.
Then he would be done.
Charlie reached into his wallet
And pulled out a folded yellow card.
It had a list of scriptures
To read when times are hard.
My demeanor began to soften,
For I knew this encounter was divine.
It was all about God's agenda
And little to do with mine.
This man began to share his story:
How he smoked and drank too much.
He described himself as a sinner
In need of a delivering touch.
At this point, my heart was engaged,

For I understood His search.
It had nothing to do with a quarter.
Charlie needed the church,
Where he could gain understanding
And learn better how to cope,
Grow closer to the living God,
Who offers a future with hope.
I shared a scripture with Charlie
And gave him a Sunday school book.
At some point during the day
He promised to take a look.
I invited him to fellowship
With our congregation next week.
He said he would be there,
For a change he desired to seek.
As we concluded our visit,
We took a moment to pray,
Beseeching the Lord for guidance
And strength to face each day.
Lord, thank You for allowing
My life to be a light
To remind a man named Charlie
He is precious in Your sight.

"Then the master said to the servant, 'Go out into the highways and hedges, and compel them to come in, that my house may be filled.'" Luke 14:23

Changing of the Guard

When braids turn into a bouffant
And black hair fades to gray,
The hands of time serve notice
A change is on the way.
When those who were once caregivers
Will rely on others to care,
Do not ignore their plight
As if they were not there.
Some age with grace never showing
Their actual number of years,
While others experience pain
That prompts the shedding of tears.
As their gait becomes unsteady,
Barely able to shuffle along,
They cringe, recalling the past
When they were agile and strong.
As we strive to render support,
How do we make them feel
While fixing their plate at supper
Or dispensing the next pill?
In spite of the demands in this season,
We do well not to forget
Each sacrifice made for us
When they gave without regret.

"Even to your old age and gray hairs I am He, I am He who will sustain you. I have made you and I will carry you; I will sustain you and I will rescue you." Isaiah 46:4

Who Else but GOD?

Hallelujah! Thank you, Jesus!
Need I say it again?
Hallelujah! Thank you, Jesus!
Yes and Amen!
Lord, you know my heart,
When it is heavy and light.
An infinitely wise Savior,
Who makes everything right!
Thank you for good rest
And for waking me up.
Thank you for the blessing
Of an overflowing cup.
Am I a millionaire?
No, not yet.
But I have wealth in knowing
There is no need to fret.
My God sits high,
Yet He always looks low,
Watching over me
Everywhere I go.
His grace is sufficient.
His mercy is rich,
Present to help me
With nary a hitch!

"Have you not known? Have you not heard? The everlasting God, the Lord, the Creator of the ends of the earth, neither faints nor is weary. His understanding is unsearchable. He gives power to the weak, and to those who have no might He increases strength." Isaiah 40:28-29

Refuge

When trouble is all around,
Rocking you to and fro,
Increasing fear and doubt,
Where will you go?
Do you seek the help of friends
With problems of their own,
Hoping they will listen
As you chatter away and moan?
Whatever you are facing,
The Lord is on your side.
In Him there is salvation
For all who choose to abide,
So instead of looking to others
For the peace you hope to find,
Put your confidence in the Lord
To ease your restless mind.

"But You, O LORD, are a shield for me, my glory and the One who lifts up my head. Salvation belongs to the LORD. Your blessing is upon Your people. Selah." Psalm 3:3, 8

Choices

When you wake up from sleeping,
And the world is beckoning you
To seek unfruitful pleasures,
What will you decide to do?
Although The LORD is almighty
And worthy of respect,
He will not make you serve Him
When you choose to rebel or object.
While sin can be inviting,
It is hardly worth the cost
Of yielding to temptation
And being eternally lost.

"And do this, knowing the time, that now it is high time to awake out of sleep; for now our salvation is nearer than when we first believed. The night is far spent, the day is at hand. Therefore let us cast off the works of darkness, and let us put on the armor of light. Let us walk properly, as in the day, not in revelry and drunkenness, not in lewdness and lust, not in strife and envy. But put on the Lord Jesus Christ, and make no provision for the flesh, to fulfill its lusts." Romans 13:11-14

Heed and Succeed

Look and learn.
Do not repeat!
See the fruit of my error.
Then turn and retreat!
From my mistakes
Heed the lesson taught:
Reckless living
Will surely come to naught!
Oh, but grace
Abundant and free
Poured out from heaven
To save a wretch like me!
Securing my redemption
From the pit of a burning Hell
By Jesus Christ the Lord
In Whom I now prevail!

"For sin shall not have dominion over you, for you are not under law but under grace. What then? Shall we sin because we are not under law but under grace? Certainly not! Do you not know that to whom you present yourselves slaves to obey, you are that one's slaves whom you obey, whether of sin leading to death, or of obedience leading to righteousness? But God be thanked that though you were slaves of sin, yet you obeyed from the heart that form of doctrine to which you were delivered. And having been set free from sin, you became slaves of righteousness." Romans 6:14-18

As Jesus Would

What would Jesus do?
Tell me, what would He say
To help somebody lost
Find their way?
Would He point accusingly
And spit in their face?
Or would He show mercy
While extending His grace?
Would he run down the list
Of each ungodly wrong,
Or would He encourage them
To repent and be strong?
Would Jesus run about
Here and there
Exposing their deeds
While soliciting prayer?
What do you think?
Could a *Savior* do this:
Embrace a hurting soul
With a meaningless kiss?
I feel most certain
This could never be true,
But the question to ponder is:
What will we do?

"Brethren, if a man is overtaken in any trespass, you who are spiritual restore such a one in a spirit of gentleness, considering yourself lest you also be tempted. Bear one another's burdens, and so fulfill the law of Christ. For if anyone thinks himself to be something, when he is nothing, he deceives himself." Galatians 6:1-3

It Is Written

Soul food!
God's Holy Word!
Some folks despise
And simply find it absurd.
But I am most convinced
This holy record is true
And what is stated therein
My God is able to do:
Scatter stars in the sky,
Hang the sun and moon in space;
Giving order to the universe,
Everything in just the right place!
Create a man out of clay,
Grant passage through a sea;
Allow His Son to die
For the likes of you and me;
Changing us from within
To become a new creation;
Sharing His message of love
To people of every nation.
Because God is not willing
That anyone should perish.
For whom He created
God truly does cherish!

"And so we have the prophetic word confirmed, which you do well to heed as a light that shines in a dark place, until the day dawns and the morning star rises in your hearts; knowing this first, that no prophecy of Scripture is of any private interpretation, for prophecy never came by the will of man, but holy men of God spoke as they were moved by the Holy Spirit." 2 Peter 1:19-21

Love for Life

When we are Humpty and Dumpty
Instead of Barbie and Ken,
Will you be able to see
The beauty I have within?
Although my coke-bottle frame
Is more like a two-liter bottle,
And my sensuous, come-hither sway
Has become a jiggle and waddle,
I am still that precious soul
You came to know and love
When we were most inseparable
And fit like a hand in glove.
In my mind I so remember,
The confidence in your walk
And the tenor of your voice
Whenever we would talk.
Despite how you change with time,
You are still the best by far.
To me you will always be
As radiant as a star!

"Like an apple tree among the trees of the wood, so is my beloved among the sons. I sat down in his shade with great delight, and his fruit was sweet to my taste." Song of Solomon 2:3

Stay in the Sheepfold

Sheep without a shepherd
Are bound to go astray,
Seeking forbidden pastures,
Refusing to obey;
Ending up in trouble,
Pursued by ravenous beasts;
Eager for a chance
To have a lamb-chop feast!
Oh, what a sinking feeling
That this could be the fate
Of those who stray beyond
The Shepherd's protective gate,
Designed to keep us safe
From the enemy lurking about,
Waiting for opportunity
To draw the lost sheep out,
Leading them to a place
They were never meant to be,
Robbing them of a future
Christ died for all to see!

"'Most assuredly, I say to you, he who does not enter the sheepfold by the door, but climbs up some other way, the same is a thief and a robber. But he who enters by the door is the shepherd of the sheep. To him the doorkeeper opens, and the sheep hear his voice; and he calls his own sheep by name and leads them out. And when he brings out his own sheep, he goes before them; and the sheep follow him, for they know his voice. Yet they will by no means follow a stranger, but will flee from him, for they do not know the voice of strangers.' Jesus used this illustration, but they did not understand the things which He spoke to them. Then Jesus said to them again, 'Most assuredly, I say to you, I am the door of the sheep. All who ever came before Me are thieves and robbers, but the

sheep did not hear them. I am the Door. If anyone enters by Me, he will be saved, and will go in and out and find pasture. The thief does not come except to steal, and to kill, and to destroy. I have come that they may have life, and that they may have it more abundantly.'" John 10:1-10

Wait and See

Do not be discouraged
By what you may see,
For things that are current
Will not always be.
Change will come
But hardly overnight,
Even when we pray
With all of our might.
Hold fast to your dreams
And watch them come true,
For what God has purposed
Will come to pass for you.

Consider Abraham: "Who against hope believed in hope, that he might become the father of many nations, according to that which was spoken, so shall your descendants be. And being not weak in faith, he considered not his own body as now dead, when he was about a hundred years old, neither yet the deadness of Sarah's womb: He staggered not at the promise of God through unbelief; but was strong in faith, giving glory to God; and being fully persuaded that, what He had promised, He was able also to perform." Romans 4:18-21

A Lesson of Love

When love that seemed so right
Starts to go terribly wrong,
You soon begin to realize
It was never really that strong.
No need racking your brain
Trying to figure things out.
Just chalk it up to experience;
No time to moan or pout.
God always knows best.
He can see what lies ahead.
His plan for you is good,
Not a life filled with dread.
If this has been your fate
Try not to feel blue,
But get ready for the blessing
God has prepared for you!

"So Boaz took Ruth, and she was his wife: and when he went in unto her, the LORD gave her conception, and she bore a son. And the women said unto Naomi, Blessed be the LORD, who has not left you this day without a kinsman, that his name may be famous in Israel." Ruth 4:13-14

The Voice of Wisdom

Hear the voice of wisdom
Crying in the street:
"Seek me! Find me!
I'll make your life sweet!
I'll give you understanding
Where you have been remiss
And help you realize
Ignorance is *not* bliss!"

When so-called friends entice you
To follow the path of sin,
Heed the voice of wisdom,
And do not enter in.
For what they fail to mention
Are the consequences in place
When you indulge in evil
And trample on God's grace.

If we would pay attention
When wisdom comes to call,
Our lives would surely reflect
What The Father wants for all:
Ever increasing knowledge
To prosper in all of our ways,
Finding joy and peace everlasting
By serving Him all of our days.

"Wisdom calls aloud outside; she raises her voice in the open squares. She cries out in the chief concourses, at the openings of the gates in the city she speaks her words: 'How long, you simple ones, will you love simplicity? For scorners delight in their scorning, and fools hate knowledge. Turn at my rebuke; surely I will pour out my spirit on you; I will make my words known to you.'" Proverbs 1:20-23

True Wealth

A king has great influence,
Powerful and bold.
His realm is far-reaching,
Full of riches untold.
Yet with all of his fortune
That delights the eye,
He would likely trade it all
To live and not die,
For of all the earthly treasures,
The greatest forms of wealth
Are to have a sound mind
And be in good health.

"Beloved, I wish above all things that you may prosper and be in health, even as your soul prospers." 3 John 1:2

Hope in Loss

Losing someone you love
Is difficult to take.
Seeing them languish in pain
Will cause intense heartache.
You long to ease their suffering
Just make it go away.
If only you could have one wish,
You would ask that they be okay.
When facing what seems to be hopeless,
Look to God and cast your care.
Although you cannot see Him,
Please trust He will be there,
Ready to bring you comfort
And reassure your soul,
Though sickness may end this life,
You will enter eternity whole!

"Blessed are they that mourn: for they shall be comforted." Matthew 5:4
"And the ransomed of the LORD shall return, and come to Zion with songs and everlasting joy upon their heads: they shall obtain joy and gladness, and sorrow and sighing shall flee away." Isaiah 35:10

The Bridge

Our Bridge over troubled water
Is always standing by
To calm an anxious spirit
And comfort us when we cry.
Nary will there be a time
When this Bridge is not in place
To heal our grieving souls
And surround us with God's grace.

"The Lord also will be a refuge for the oppressed, a refuge in times of trouble. And those who know Your name will put their trust in You; for You, Lord, have not forsaken those who seek You." Psalm 9:9-10

Silent Plea

Lord of all, infinite God,
Please hear my silent prayers.
Incline your ears to listen
As I cast away my cares.
I have no grievous complaints,
Just a few things on my mind.
I could use some Fatherly advice,
If you would be so kind.
With confidence, I shall wait
For an answer to my plea
And praise you in advance
For coming to see about me.

"O send out Your light and Your truth! Let them lead me; let them bring me to Your holy hill, and to Your tabernacle. Then will I go to the altar of God, to God my exceeding joy: and on the harp I will praise you, O God, my God. Why are you cast down, O my soul? And why are you disquieted within me? Hope in God; for I shall yet praise Him, the help of my countenance and my God." Psalm 43:3-5

Mighty Avenger

We all have mountains to climb.
We all have giants to face.
Sometimes tribulation in life
Comes at an exorbitant pace,
Creating overwhelming frustration
As we tally up the cost,
Causing our minds to wander,
Believing all hope is lost.
Who will slay this giant
That comes against us strong,
Breathing out murderous threats
And vowing to do us wrong?
Who else but our God
Is capable of this feat?
He is our mighty avenger.
In Him, there is no deceit.
When we take God at His word
And find our refuge in Him,
We are certain to overcome,
Even when chances look slim.

"Then David said to the Philistine, 'You come to me with a sword, with a spear, and with a javelin. But I come to you in the name of the Lord of hosts, the God of the armies of Israel, whom you have defied. This day the Lord will deliver you into my hand, and I will strike you and take your head from you. And this day I will give the carcasses of the camp of the Philistines to the birds of the air and the wild beasts of the earth, that all the earth may know that there is a God in Israel. Then all this assembly shall know that the Lord does not save with sword and spear; for the battle is the Lord's, and He will give you into our hands." 1 Samuel 17:45-47

Never Alone

For all the times you thought
You would not make it through,
And you felt a close presence,
Like someone embracing you,
Shielding you from harm
And dangers yet unseen,
Encouraging you to press in
When times were hard and lean,
God was there in the midst of it all,
Guiding each step of the way,
Preparing you to lay hold
Of a new and brighter day.
Behold! This is your Genesis!
A remarkable beginning!
Stand tall and walk with assurance,
For this is your season of winning.

"O Lord, You are the portion of my inheritance and my cup; You maintain my lot. The lines have fallen to me in pleasant places; yes, I have a good inheritance. I will bless the Lord who has given me counsel; My heart also instructs me in the night seasons. I have set the Lord always before me; because He is at my right hand I shall not be moved. Therefore my heart is glad, and my glory rejoices; my flesh also will rest in hope." Psalm 16:5-9

Content in HIM

Time spent with God
Is time well spent.
Through Him we know
The joy of being content,
For He teaches us to rest
And depend on Him,
Instead of being wooed
By every fickle whim.
Feasting on His word
Provides food for the soul
To nurture our spirits
And make us whole.
As we are stoked
Like logs on a fire,
Our hearts begin to burn
With increasing desire
To know God better,
More and more each day,
As we humbly submit
And choose to obey!

"My soul, wait you only upon God; for my expectation is from Him. He only is my rock and my salvation: He is my defense; I shall not be moved. In God is my salvation and my glory: the rock of my strength, and my refuge, is in God. Trust in Him at all times; you people, pour out your heart before Him: God is a refuge for us. Selah." Psalm 62:5-8

Let HIM Drive

If you ask Jesus to take the wheel,
Have faith to let Him drive,
For He knows the best direction
And the time you should arrive.
With Him, there will be no detour,
Unintentional stops or delay.
When your path is divinely ordered,
He guides you all the way.

"You shall observe to do therefore as the LORD your God has commanded you: you shall not turn aside to the right hand or to the left. You shall walk in all the ways which the LORD your God has commanded you, that you may live, and that it may be well with you, and that you may prolong your days in the land which you shall possess." Deuteronomy 5:32-33

Words

The earth is filled with words:

Words we speak,
Words we think,
Words we write down
On paper with ink;

Words that curse,
Words that bless,
Words that condemn,
Or produce happiness;

Words that destroy,
Words that breathe life,
Words that cause pain
And cut like a knife;

Words that deplete,
Words that restore,
Words that repel
Or leave us wanting more.

Words are powerful!
They can whisper a message of hope
In the midst of fear and doubt
When we find it hard to cope.

Instead of using our words,
To degrade a sister or brother,
We should strive to dwell in peace
And encourage one another.

"There is one who speaks rashly, like a piercing sword; but the tongue of the wise brings healing." Proverbs 12:18

Any Given Moment

At this appointed time,
God already knew
Where we would be
And what we would do;
How we would act
And what we would say
At any given moment
Throughout the day.
He knew what thoughts
Would come to mind,
Whether they be good
Or not so kind.
Whatever our choice,
His will is to bless.
He sees our potential
In spite of our mess.
He is never alarmed
When we make a mistake.
His grace is available,
Free for all to partake.
He does not forsake us
As other people do
But extends new mercies
To bring us through.

"O Lord, You have searched me and known me. You know my sitting down and my rising up; You understand my thought afar off. You comprehend my path and my lying down, and are acquainted with all my ways. For there is not a word on my tongue, but behold, O Lord, You know it altogether. You have hedged me behind and before, and laid Your hand upon me. Such knowledge is too wonderful for me; it is high, I cannot attain it." Psalm 139:1-6

Motherhood

Being a mother has taught me
Many wonderful things
About unconditional love
And the acceptance it brings;

On pain and pleasure
From watching my children grow
As they learn from mistakes
While choosing which way to go.

I have experienced the pride
Of seeing what they could do,
As their strengths and abilities
Invariably come shining through.

I have learned the power of prayer
And to do so without ceasing,
Particularly as the evil of the day
Seems to be ever increasing.

I ask God to help them
Stay focused and make the right choice,
To experience life in abundance
As they learn how to rejoice

In what the Lord has done
And give Him first place,
So they are endued with power
To finish this earthly race.

For He alone is their source
To supply each and every need,
As they choose to live for Him,
I know they will succeed.

[Love] "Bears all things, believes all things, hopes all things, and endures all things." 1 Corinthians 13:7
"And you shall love the LORD your God with all your heart, and with all your soul, and with all your might. And these words which I command you today shall be in your heart. You shall teach them diligently to your children, and shall talk of them when you sit in your house, and when you walk by the way, when you lie down, and when you rise. You shall bind them as a sign on your hand, and they shall be as frontlets between your eyes." Deuteronomy 6:5-8

While You Wait

While waiting on your change to come,
Give God praise!
For when you least expect it,
His wonders will amaze.
To grant your heart's desire
As you delight in Him;
Instead of chasing fantasies
That leave you out on a limb.
You need not be anxious;
His timing is impeccable.
You need not question how;
His ways are unsearchable!

"O the depth of the riches both of the wisdom and knowledge of God! How unsearchable are His judgments, and His ways past finding out!" Romans 11:33

Church Lady

"Church Lady, Church Lady, please lend me your ears!
My burdens are heavy, and I'm almost in tears!"

"I'm sorry, Miss, but I'm off to a meeting.
I'll call you tonight, once I've finished eating."

"But Church Lady, please, I'm at the end of my rope!"

"Well, here, read this pamphlet; it will tell you how to cope:"

Ten Easy Ways to Reduce Stress, When Your Life Is a Hot Mess!

"This is going to fix me? Make my problems go away?"

"Perhaps if you read it. What more is there to say?"

"There must be something more to this God you talk about,
The one who makes you dance, moan, testify, and shout."
Does He not have time for one such as me?
Or is He like you, too busy to hear my plea?"

"Like me, too busy? Well that is just not true!
Please try to understand I simply have things to do."

"More important than MY child, who is standing here in need?
If you are truly MY disciple, show ME by your deeds!
You are MY hands, and you are MY feet.
I have filled you with MY Spirit to be light for those you meet,
Who stand in darkness, struggling to come out.
Show them MY love to dispel fear and doubt!"

"Oh, Miss, just a moment; I do have time to spare.
I didn't mean to be hasty as if I didn't care.

God's love is amazing! He wants the best for all.
He listens to our prayers and answers when we call.
His greatest act of love was to send His only Son,
Jesus Christ, The Messiah; He died for everyone
To free us from a life of misery and shame.
Ask Him in your heart, and you'll never be the same!"

"Dear God, I need You; please come and take control;
Deliver me from sin and heal my wounded soul.
Show me the good I was created to do
As I live in a way that is pleasing to you.
Relieve me of pain, sadness, and strife
Unto Your Son, Jesus, I commend my life."

"Well Miss, tell me how do you feel?
Can you now sense that God is real?"

"Yes, and thank you for sharing with me
God's love and how He saves abundantly."

"Brethren, if anyone among you wanders from the truth, and someone turns him back, let him know that he who turns a sinner from the error of his way will save a soul from death and cover a multitude of sins."
James 5:19-20

Intercession

In obedience and faith,
I kneel in prayer,
Believing that God
Will meet me there,
Attentive and waiting
To hear my request,
Prepared to answer
As only He knows best.
"Lord, I come before You,
Humble as I know how;
Beseeching You for healing
Of Your servant now.
He knows you have been good to him
Every year, month, and day.
He knows without a doubt
You have kept him all the way.
He has no complaints,
In spite of sickness and pain,
So I ask on his behalf
For good health to come again.
Lord, You know the illness,
And You know the cure.
Please grant him strength
And a will to endure.
Lord, send Your power
From heaven on high.
As I pray with assurance,
Make haste to draw nigh."
I ask it all in Jesus' name. Amen!

"Praying at all times in the Spirit, with all prayer and supplication. To that end keep alert with all perseverance, making supplication for all the saints." Ephesians 6:18

Good as New

Left work feeling rather weighted and tired,
But as I looked in The Word, I was lifted and inspired.
God's word is good; Mmmm, yummy, eat it up!
Take a deep drink from an overflowing cup.
Looking at the woman with an issue of blood,
An outcast of society treated like mud.
She pressed her way through the crowd,
A little nervous but not too proud
To reach the One who could change her life
And deliver her from suffering and strife.
This woman had faith to be made whole
While securing redemption for her soul.
Like this woman we should be as bold
And seek the Savior as pure gold.
In Him we become our absolute best,
For our Lord gives power to pass every test.

"Yet the Lord longs to be gracious to you; He rises to show you compassion. For the Lord is a God of justice. Blessed are all who wait for Him! People of Zion who live in Jerusalem, you will weep no more. How gracious He will be when you cry for help. As soon as He hears, He will answer you." Isaiah 30:18-19

The Man in the Median

I saw a man in the median
After leaving Columbia Mall,
Somewhat average looking,
Lean, and rather tall.
He was waving a sign
As motorists passed by.
When I saw what was written,
I could not help but reply.
A one-word statement,
It simply read: "SMILE."
Of all the signs out there,
This one was so worthwhile.
As I complied with his directive,
The man gave a shout,
Saying, "Oh yeah,
That's what I'm talking about!"
My daughter stated laughing
When he spoke out loud.
I laughed a bit myself
As he danced and bowed.
This funny little gesture
In a most peculiar place
Came at just the right time
To put a smile on my face.

"But let the righteous be glad; let them rejoice before God: yes, let them rejoice exceedingly." Psalm 68:3

A Friend in Deed

A friend is there
Through thick and thin
To encourage you
Not to give in
When life starts to get
A little too rough,
And you think your best
Is never good enough.
A friend is aware
You have what it takes
To keep moving forward
In spite of mistakes.
There is no length
A friend will not go
To build you up
So you can grow
Beyond your circumstance,
Whatever it may be,
So you can find purpose
By achieving your destiny!

"Just as iron sharpens iron, a person sharpens the character of his friend."
Proverbs 27:17

Diving into Destiny

Standing on a diving board
High above a pool,
Nervous as anyone could be,
Trying to play it cool.
The water seemed so far away,
Immense, deep, and cold.
I knew I needed to jump on in,
But could I be so bold?
I thought about my form.
Would it look all right?
I wanted it to be flawless
And graceful as an eagle in flight.
I considered all the people
Watching from below:
Were they present to encourage me
Or just hoping to see a good show?
At last, I concluded,
However my feat turned out,
It was time to get moving
And stop standing about.
I closed my eyes tight
And briefly whispered a prayer:
"Lord, when I reach the bottom,
I know You will be there
To guide me through the water
Until I rise on top.
Even if my form
Turns out to be a flop."

Now, with eyes wide open,
I am ready to begin
The race that lies before me
And quite determined to win.

"Whenever I am afraid, I will trust in you." Psalm 56:3

No Offense

If someone treats you wrong,
You need not think twice.
Instead of seeking revenge,
Try extra hard to be nice.
Although it would be easy
To return behavior in kind,
It would not please God,
Nor give you peace of mind.
So when temptation comes,
Refuse to give it place,
But rather be an example
Of God's magnificent grace.

"Do not repay evil with evil or insult with insult. On the contrary, repay evil with blessing, because to this you were called so that you may inherit a blessing." 1 Peter 3:9

Choices and Voices

Choices and voices:
Which road will you take?
Who will you give ear to?
What decision will you make?
Many will form an opinion
On what is best for you,
But only God knows
What you were created to do.
If you take the easy route,
Those who join you there
Will likely have your back
As long as the weather is fair.

When you decide to change
And yearn for something more,
The road you now must travel
To some may be a bore.

"Come on, let's kick it!
Turn up and get down!
There's a party just starting
On the other side of town.
Say what? You have *Bible* study?
What for? That ain't no fun!
You be strong, but as for me,
I'm out. Gotta run!"

Now you hear the voices.
They beckon you to give in:
"Just once more, for old time's sake.
What's wrong with a *little* sin?"

Even when your associates
Leave you hanging high and dry,
Discern the voice of The Father
And know that He is nigh:

"Be strong and of good courage,
Have faith and trust in me,
For I will never leave,
Nor will I forsake thee!"

So when it comes to choices,
Take heed of sage advice.
Once determined to live holy,
Refuse to think twice.

"My son, if you receive my words, and treasure my commands within you, so that you incline your ear to wisdom, and apply your heart to understanding; yes, if you cry out for discernment, and lift up your voice for understanding, if you seek her as silver, and search for her as for hidden treasures; then you will understand the fear of the Lord, and find the knowledge of God." Proverbs 2:1-5

Wisdom and Revelation

Fresh oil pouring out
To feed my spirit man,
Showing me what is to be,
According to God's plan.
I hear The Word; it speaks to me,
Encouraging me to be strong;
Leading me on the path
To discover where I belong.
Standing in His presence,
It all seems very clear;
My hopes, dreams, and purpose
Are beginning to appear.
The more I learn about
The One who created me,
The more I understand
How glorious life can be.
As I continue to seek Him
And in His will abide,
The stronger the gifts become
My God has placed inside!

"As each one has received a gift, minister it to one another, as good stewards of the manifold grace of God. If anyone speaks, let him speak as the oracles of God. If anyone ministers, let him do it as with the ability which God supplies, that in all things God may be glorified through Jesus Christ, to whom belong the glory and the dominion forever and ever. Amen." 1 Peter 4:10-11

Girlfriends

Thank God for girlfriends
Who know just what to do
When life events happen
To get the best of you.

They know how to listen
While you state your mind,
To offer sage advice,
Speaking genuinely and kind.

And even better yet
Is a girlfriend who can pray,
Crying out to God on your behalf
When you are not sure what to say.

God bless these dear ladies
Who willingly intercede
To promote the welfare of others
They perceive to be in need.

"The heart is delighted by the fragrance of oil and sweet perfumes, and in just the same way, the soul is sweetened by the wise counsel of a friend."
Proverbs 27:9

Service with a Smile

Breakfast and a meeting
At a local joint.
Prior to beginning
Someone made it a point
To read a meditation
In order to set the mood
Before delving into business
Or eating any food.
The passage read reminded us
The Lord made this day;
Thus we should rejoice and be glad
In what we do or say.
As we sat in the corner,
A semi-cozy spot,
Our waitress plopped down
A second coffee pot:
"Are you ready to order?"
Her interjection came quick.
"Just a little more time,"
As we had yet to pick.
She returned awhile later,
Ready to take our requests;
She seemed a bit annoyed.
Was she not feeling her best?
Taking our orders with haste,
Then making her exit swift,
Her demeanor made us think
Perhaps her spirits needed a lift.
Returning with our food
She rapidly dealt each plate.
We all felt her service
Was far from being great.
Admittedly, we were annoyed,

But we decided to be nice.
In reflection of our meditation,
Anything less would not suffice.
It was learned a bit later
Our waitress was feeling okay.
She was just overwhelmed
From having a busy day.
In planning our next meeting,
We will probably meet elsewhere.
Nonetheless, we shall keep
Our dear waitress lifted in prayer.

"See that no one renders evil for evil to anyone, but always pursue what is good both for yourselves and for all. Rejoice always, pray without ceasing, and in everything give thanks; for this is the will of God in Christ Jesus for you." 1 Thessalonians 5:15-18

About Easter

Easter Sunday,
Resurrection Day,
A time set aside to celebrate
The love God sent our way.

Embodied in our Savior,
The Lord Jesus Christ.
His death upon the cross
Was the ultimate sacrifice.

High on Calvary's Mountain
He hung for all to see.
His blood came streaming down,
Poured out for you and me.
Now Joseph of Arimathea,
A good and just man,
Requested the body of Jesus
To fulfill his part in God's plan.

He wrapped His body in linen,
Then laid Him in the tomb.
The lifeless body of Jesus
Seemingly had met its doom.

The women who followed Jesus
Stood watching from nearby,
Making plans to return after Sabbath
With spices and fragrance to apply.

All night He lay in the tomb;
Then came the morning light.
When the women arrived to anoint Him,
Jesus was nowhere in sight!

Two men appeared in bright raiment
To explain Jesus did what He said:
"He is not here, for He has risen.
Why seek the living among the dead?"

So the women left rejoicing,
For they had a story to tell
About Jesus, the Risen Messiah,
Whom they had loved so well.

Like them, we too have reason
To rejoice in what Jesus has done.
He was obedient unto death
To bring salvation to everyone.

"But on the first day of the week, at early dawn, they went to the tomb, taking the spices they had prepared. And they found the stone rolled away from the tomb, but when they went in they did not find the body of the Lord Jesus. While they were perplexed about this, behold, two men stood by them in dazzling apparel. And as they were frightened and bowed their faces to the ground, the men said to them, "Why do you seek the living among the dead? He is not here, but has risen. Remember how he told you, while he was still in Galilee, that the Son of Man must be delivered into the hands of sinful men and be crucified and on the third day rise." And they remembered his words." Luke 24:1-8

Good Friday

In recognition of Good Friday,
I thought to pen a poem
To reflect on the cost of salvation
That grants us a heavenly home.

Now Jesus, speaking with His disciples,
Encouraged them to be of good cheer;
He knew they would all be scattered,
For the hour was drawing near.

Although He would soon be abandoned,
Jesus knew He was not alone.
The Father who sent Him from Heaven
Would bring glory to His Own.

As they entered into the garden,
Jesus, aware of His fate,
Approached the one who betrayed Him,
Standing with soldiers in wait.

Then Judas stepped out from among them
For a sign they could not miss.
As he placed his arms around Jesus,
He embraced Him with a kiss.

Simon Peter, His zealous disciple,
Who denied Jesus thrice,
Drew his sword against a soldier
And severed his ear with a slice.

After healing the wounded man,
Jesus was taken by force
To stand before the high priest,
Who waivered their plan with remorse.

Once Jesus was savagely beaten,
They crowned His head with thorns,
Then cloaked Him in a robe of purple,
As the people beheld Him with scorn.

His trial was swiftly concluded
By the crowd with alarming resound,
Shouting for Pilate to "Crucify Him,"
Although no fault was found.

They marched Him to Golgotha,
Where He was crucified.
Two thieves worthy of death
Were placed on either side.

Although Jesus did no wrong,
He endured a cross of shame
For the redemption of lost mankind
And the Kingdom of God to proclaim.

"But Jesus answered them, saying, "The hour has come that the Son of Man should be glorified. Most assuredly, I say to you, unless a grain of wheat falls into the ground and dies, it remains alone; but if it dies, it produces much grain. He who loves his life will lose it, and he who hates his life in this world will keep it for eternal life. If anyone serves Me, let him follow Me; and where I am, there My servant will be also. If anyone serves Me, him My Father will honor." John 12:23-26

The Tongue

Who can tame an unruly tongue?
An instrument by which many are hung.
Such a small thing, but strong as an ox,
Loaded with venom and sly as a fox!
A chameleon of sorts, with a dual role
That can rock your world or soothe the soul.
It can rip you to shreds like a whip,
Then pour out words that are honey dipped!
What can be done to subdue this foe,
So the fruit it yields helps others to grow?
Cry out to God to have His way
And ask for guidance in what to say.
Find delight in giving others a break
When they cause you harm or make a mistake.
Then take the time to read and study God's word,
So you walk upright and not seem absurd.

> *"But no man can tame the tongue. It is an unruly evil, full of deadly poison. With it we bless our God and Father, and with it we curse men, who have been made in the similitude of God. Out of the same mouth proceed blessing and cursing. My brethren, these things ought not to be so… Who is wise and understanding among you? Let him show by good conduct that his works are done in the meekness of wisdom." James 3:8-10; 13*

Crossing Over

On the bridge of life,
Betwixt and between,
Trying to decide
On which side you should lean:
Toward the former things
That led you to choose wrong
Or on the side of Christ,
Where you belong.
He sees your potential
In the midst of your mistakes.
Regardless of your past,
You have what it takes
To rise above a lifestyle
Filled with pain and despair,
To become more than a conqueror
Surrounded by His care,
So when you feel the old man
Trying to pull you back,
Look to the joy that lies ahead,
And you will stay on track.

"And this I pray, that your love may abound still more and more in knowledge and all discernment, that you may approve the things that are excellent, that you may be sincere and without offense till the day of Christ, filled with the fruits of righteousness which are by Jesus Christ, to the glory and praise of God." Philippians 1:9-11

More Than You See

Behind the "Scarlet Letter"
Beats the heart of a wounded soul
Whom God sees great potential in,
Once they are made whole.
Amid the guilt and shame of sin
It is difficult to see
The beauty that resides within
And who you are meant to be.
If ever you feel your fate is sealed
And your life is beyond repair,
Cry out to the Savior for help,
And He will be right there
To restore your hopes and dreams
Abandoned along the way
And place you on a path
That leads to a brighter day.

"Create in me a clean heart, O God, and renew a right spirit within me. Cast me not away from Your presence, and take not Your Holy Spirit from me. Restore to me the joy of Your salvation, and uphold me by Your generous Spirit. Then I will teach transgressors Your ways, and sinners shall be converted to You." Psalm 51:10-13

Our Help

When you find yourself in the valley,
Overwhelmed by a load of care,
Lift your eyes toward the heavens
And remember God is there,
"A very present help in trouble,"
Our "Rock in a weary land."
If we should stumble or fall,
His strength will help us stand.
We can trust Him to provide daily
To meet our every need,
And as we delight in His word,
He positions us to succeed.
Is anything too hard for God?
No! Not at all!
For He hears our faintest cry,
And He answers when we call.

"Let my cry come before You, O Lord; give me understanding according to Your word. Let my supplication come before You; deliver me according to Your word. My lips shall utter praise, for You teach me Your statutes. My tongue shall speak of Your word, for all Your commandments are righteousness. Let Your hand become my help, for I have chosen Your precepts. I long for Your salvation, O Lord, and Your law is my delight." Psalm 119:169-174

Hidden Treasure

There is a treasure in this vessel
The enemy wants to steal
To keep us from becoming
Whom God wants to reveal.
He wants to create worry
And whisper words of doubt.
He wants us to believe
There is just no way out.
But God has made provision
To thwart the enemy's scheme
And keep him from destroying
All our hopes and dreams.
For in His Dear Son, Jesus,
Who died to save us all,
We have the gift of salvation
Whenever we choose to call.
And as we seek Him daily,
He leads us along the way
And showers us with blessings
As we trust Him and obey.

"I will go before you and make the crooked places straight; I will break in pieces the gates of bronze and cut the bars of iron. I will give you the treasures of darkness and hidden riches of secret places, that you may know that I, the Lord, Who call you by your name, Am the God of Israel." Isaiah 45:2-3

Mercy

When Jesus encountered the woman
Caught in an adulterous act,
He did not disregard it,
Nor did He overreact.
With eyes of great compassion,
He looked beyond her plight.
Then kneeling in the dirt
Jesus began to write.
Exactly what was written
One can only speculate,
But whatever He spelled out
Gave cause to contemplate,
For slowly one by one
The crowd began to disband,
And as they walked away,
Rocks fell from their hands.
What a poignant moment,
That woman and Jesus alone.
What was He going to say
Now that the crowd had gone?
"As no one stands to condemn you,
Henceforth, neither do I."
With great relief and wonder,
She breathed a heavy sigh.
"Go now and leave your life of sin
And put your trust in Me,
For I will be your strength to stand
And make your enemies flee."

"Jesus stood up and said to her, "Woman, where are they? Has no one condemned you?" She said, "No one, Lord." And Jesus said, "Neither do I condemn you; go and sin no more." John 8:10-11

About the Author

Marcia Y. Collins is a native resident of Columbia, Missouri. She discovered an affinity for writing at an early age and soon realized she had a particular gift for writing poetry. Throughout her lifetime, Marcia has written numerous poems. It was after chronicling her treatment for breast cancer that she began to consider putting a collection together to encourage others facing life challenges. She is thrilled to see her dream of publishing come to fruition and looks forward to completing more projects in the future.

Acknowledgments

I want to express my appreciation to everyone who helped make my dream of publishing this book a reality. Every dollar given, every encouraging word, every response on Facebook, and each gentle nudge meant to keep me on task has helped me realize how much I have to be grateful for.

Last but not least, I thank God, our creator and the giver of *every good and perfect gift,* for placing in me the ability to write, and providing an opportunity to share it with others. This project has taught me to believe that everyone has purpose, and is filled with potential to do the incredible if given the chance. It is never too late to leave a legacy others can benefit from. Thank you all!

www.ingramcontent.com/pod-product-compliance
Lightning Source LLC
Chambersburg PA
CBHW031321160426
43196CB00007B/614